Somaly Mam is president and spokesperson of the Somaly Mam Foundation and is one of the most prolific activists fighting sexual slavery today. Somaly was one of the founding members of AFESIP – Acting for Women in Distressing Circumstances – an organisation which has rescued, rehabilitated and reintegrated over 4,000 women and children since its inception in 1996. Somaly Mam has been the recipient of several awards including *Glamour* magazine Woman of the Year for 2006, CNN Hero, as well as recognition from the U.S. Department of Homeland Security.

The Road of
Lost Innocence

The True Story of a Cambodian Childhood

SOMALY MAM

Translated from the French by
LISA APPIGNANESI

virago

VIRAGO

First published in Great Britain by Virago Press in 2007
This edition published by Virago Press in 2008

Originally published in France in 2005 under the title
Le silence de l'innocence
Copyright © Editions Anne Carrière, Paris, 2005

The right of Somaly Mam to be identified as the author of this
Work has been asserted by her in accordance with the
Copyright, Designs and Patents Act 1988

A CIP catalogue record for this book
is available from the British Library.

ISBN 978-1-84408-346-6

Typeset in Sabon by M Rules
Printed and bound in Great Britain by
Clays Ltd, St Ives plc

Virago Press
An imprint of
Little, Brown Book Group
100 Victoria Embankment
London EC4Y 0DY

An Hachette Livre UK Company
www.hachettelivre.co.uk

www.virago.co.uk

'By far the lowest statistic for the number of prostitutes and sex slaves in Cambodia is between 40,000 and 50,000. It can be expected that at least 1 in 40 girls born in Cambodia will be sold into sex slavery.'

2005 report by The Future Group, a Canadian non-governmental organisation

In 1986, when I was sold to a brothel as a prostitute, I was about sixteen years old. Today there many far younger prostitutes in Cambodia. There are virgins for sale in every large town; to be sure of their virginity, the girls are sometimes as young as five or six.

In Cambodia, and throughout South-East Asia, tens of thousands of children are forced into prostitution each year. They are raped and beaten. Many are killed.

I dedicate this book to the thousands of little girls who are sold into prostitution every year.

Contents

For reasons of privacy, certain names
have been changed.

1

The Forest

My name is Somaly. At least, that's the name I have now. Like everyone in Cambodia, I've had several. Names are the result of temporary choices. You change them the way you'd change lives. As a small child, I was called Ya, and sometimes just Non – Little One. When I was taken away from the forest by the old man, I was called Aya, and once, at a border crossing, he told the guard my name was Viriya – I don't really know why. I got used to people calling me all sorts of names, mostly insults. Then, years later, a kind man who said he was my uncle gave me the name Somaly: 'the necklace of flowers lost in the virgin forest'. I liked it; it seemed to fit the idea of who I felt I really was. When I finally had the choice, I decided to keep that name as my own.

I will never know what my parents called me. But then I have nothing from them, no memories at all. My adoptive father once gave me this typically Khmer advice: 'You shouldn't hurt yourself. You shouldn't try to discover the past.' I suspect he knows what really happened, but he has never talked to me about it. The little I do know I've had to piece together with vague recollections and some help from history.

I spent my earliest years in the rolling countryside of north-eastern Cambodia, surrounded by savannah and forests, not far from the high plains of Vietnam. Even today, when I have the chance to go into the forest, I feel at home. I recognise smells. I recognise plants. I instinctively know what's good to eat and what's poisonous. I remember the waterfalls. The sound of them is still in my ears. We children would bathe naked under the cascading water and play at holding our breath. I remember the smell of the virgin forest. I have a buried memory of this place.

The people of Bou Sra, the village where I was born, are Phnong. They are an old tribe of mountain people, quite unlike the Khmer who dominate the lowlands of Cambodia. I have inherited the typical Phnong dark skin from my mother. Cambodians see it as black and ugly. In Khmer, the word Phnong means 'savage'. Throughout South-East Asia, people are very sensitive about skin colour. The paler you are, the closer to 'moon colour', the more highly you are prized. A plump woman with white skin is the supreme object of beauty and desire. I was dark and thin and very unattractive.

My parents left me with my maternal grandmother when I was still a small child. Perhaps they were seeking a better life, or perhaps they had been forced to leave. I was born sometime around 1970 or 1971, when the troubles began in Cambodia. Before I turned five, the country had been carpet-bombed by the Americans. Then it was seized by the murderous regime of Pol Pot's Khmer Rouge. The four years of Khmer Rouge rule, from 1975 to 1979, were responsible for the deaths of about one in five people in Cambodia through execution, starvation or forced labour. In the storm of events, countless others were simply swept away from their villages and families without leaving any trace behind. People were displaced to work camps where they worked as slaves, or were forced to fight for the regime. There are many reasons why my parents might have left the forest.

The story I like to tell myself is that my parents and grandmother always had my best interests at heart. Among the Phnong, the mother's lineage determines ethnicity. So despite my father being Khmer, when my parents left, my place was in Mondulkiri. Not long thereafter my grandmother would also be swept away; much too soon for me to have any lasting memory of her. Mountain people up and leave for any old reason, as soon as anything displeases them. No one expected an explanation, especially not during those troubled years. So when my grandmother left the forest, no one knew where she went. I don't think I was abandoned: she probably thought I'd be safest in the village with my own people. There was no way she could have known that the forest would not be my home for long.

Our village was nothing more than a dozen round huts clustered in a forest clearing. The huts were made of plaited bamboo, their straw roofs low to the ground. Most families shared a single large hut. There was no partition between the communal sleeping platform and the cooking area. Other families kept themselves separate. But with no parents or other family in the village, I would sleep on my own in a hammock. I really did live like a little savage. I slept here or there, ate where I could. I was at home everywhere and nowhere. I don't remember any other children who slept alone among the trees, as I did. No, I was the only one who did that. Perhaps I wasn't taken in by anyone because I was of mixed race – part Phnong and part Khmer. Or perhaps I just made a decision to be by myself. Being an orphan in Cambodia is no rare condition. It is frighteningly ordinary.

I wasn't generally unhappy. But I remember feeling cold all the time. On particularly bitter or rainy nights a kind man, Taman, would make space for me in his home. He was a Cham, a Muslim Khmer, but his wife was Phnong. I can't remember her name, but I thought she was beautiful with her long black hair tied behind her head with a bamboo stick, her high cheekbones and a necklace made of shiny black wood and animal teeth. She was nice to me. Sometimes she would try to wash my long hair, rubbing the ash of a special herb into it to clean it, and then oiling it with pig fat and combing it with her fingers while she sang. She wore an intricately woven black and red cloth around her waist. Some women would leave their breasts bare, but Taman's wife covered hers.

Taman, like the other men, wore a loincloth that left his buttocks bare. They wore strings of beads and bows strapped around their backs and they had thick cylinders of wood through their earlobes.

We children would be unclothed most of the time. We would play or make clothes together out of thick, flat leaves wrapped around with vines while Taman's wife would weave for hours on end, sitting on the floor with her legs stretched out in front of her and the bamboo loom tied on over her feet.

Her teeth were filed into sharp points. Phnong girls file and blacken their teeth when they become women, but I left the village long before the time for filing my teeth came.

I was always looking for a mother, so that I could be held in her arms, kissed and stroked, like Taman's wife held her children. I was very unhappy not to have a mother like everyone else. My only confidants were the trees. I talked to them and told them about my sorrow. They listened, understood and made discreet signs in my direction. They were my only true friends, alongside the moon. When things got unbearable I talked to the waterfalls; I could see that the water, to which I confessed my secrets, couldn't reverse its flow and betray me. Even today, I sometimes talk to trees. Other than that I almost never spoke as a child. There wouldn't have been much point in any case: nobody would have listened.

I found my own food. I would roam the forest and eat what I could find: fruit, wild vegetables and honey. There were also plenty of insects, such as grasshoppers and ants, to eat. I particularly loved the ants. I still know where to look up to find fruits and berries, and I still know that there are bees you can follow to find their honey. And I still know that you should look down because there are mushrooms on the ground, but also snakes.

If I caught an animal I would take it to Taman's wife to cook. She cooked meat under a layer of ash, because ash is naturally salty. Sometimes she dried the little pieces of meat in buffalo dung, mixed them with bitter herbs and rice and cooked them over the fire. When I returned to the village almost twenty-five years later and rediscovered that dish I ate so much that I made myself sick.

As the mountain land was ill suited for growing rice, the entire village had to work together. The forest had to be burned to create rice paddies. Every few years the earth would become infertile and we would be forced to go further and further afield in search of good soil. The distances were huge, especially for my little legs and sometimes we'd have to walk for several days. We had no carts or work animals of the kind the Khmer had in their flooded rice paddies, and so everything we brought back we'd have to carry ourselves.

When the rice was harvested, we would sacrifice a buffalo to the spirits who lived in the forest. People from several villages would gather around a fire to celebrate the harvest. Everyone danced to the beat of the metal gongs. There'd be endless banqueting and lots of rice wine. I remember the earthenware jars being enormous; they were almost as tall as I was. We'd drink the wine straight from the jar, one by one, sipping it up through a bamboo straw. Even we children would be allowed to join in. I remember a great deal of kindness towards the children. The Phnong people are good to children – not like the Khmer.

Our hills were so remote that probably no doctor or nurse had ever stepped foot in them. There were certainly no schools. I never saw a Buddhist or Christian preacher. And although my childhood coincided with the Khmer Rouge regime, I also have no recollection of ever seeing any soldiers.

The Khmer Rouge had decreed that mountain people like the Phnong were 'core people'. We were examples for others to follow, because we had no contact with Western habits and instead lived collectively. That, and our forests and hills, protected us from the suffering that engulfed the rest of Cambodia while I was a small child.

Pol Pot had abolished money throughout the entire country, along with school diplomas, motor vehicles, eyeglasses, books and any sign of modern life. But I don't think that's why we had no currency. The Phnong never needed money. If the grown-ups wanted something we couldn't make or grow or hunt, they traded for it. If we wanted a cabbage, we went to ask a neighbour who had planted some. He would give us one without asking for anything in return. Now it's different: the people from Phnom Penh arrive on weekends or during the holidays in their big 4x4s with their pockets full of money.

One day, when I was about nine or ten, Taman called me into his hut and introduced me to a stranger. This man, like Taman, was a Cham – a Cambodian Muslim. He was very tall and strongly built; he had a thin nose like Taman, and pale skin. I suppose he might have been about fifty-five, which is very old in Cambodia. Taman told me that this man was from the same place as my father. He used the word 'grandfather', as all Cambodians do to show respect to the elderly. He told me that if I went with this grandfather he would take me to my father's province and I would find my family.

Perhaps Taman really believed that this grandfather would take care of me. Perhaps he truly thought this old Cham man would help me find my father's relatives. Perhaps he was convinced that I would be better off living in the lowlands, with an adult to look after me. Or perhaps he sold me to this man, knowing full well that, at best, I would become his indentured servant.

I have tried many times to find Taman, to understand his reasoning, but I never have, and anyway I've since learned that it's never possible to discover what really motivates people.

At first I really liked this grandfather and was happy

to leave with him. Not many people had proposed to look after me in my short life. I thought this man was my real grandfather, someone who would adopt and love me. I thought he knew where my parents were. I put together a bundle with a tunic that Taman's wife had made for me, along with a wooden necklace and a short black and red cloth with green embroidery.

We began walking. We walked for a long time, along paths that took us further and further from the places I knew. He wasn't talkative, but neither was I. He spoke very little Phnong and we were forced to communicate with rudimentary gestures.

We came to a place where people were swarming around a giant logging truck. I couldn't understand what on earth was going on. It was the largest, most frightening thing I had ever seen. There was no way I was going to climb on the logs like everyone else – the truck terrified me. I had never even seen a bicycle before, let alone a motorised vehicle.

I backed away, but Grandfather glared at me and raised his hand menacingly. I didn't understand this gesture – I had never been hit – but I saw that his face had changed, that it was rough and angry, and it frightened me even more than the truck did. Then his hand struck me with a hard blow that knocked me to the ground. My cheek bleeding, he pulled me up and on to the truck.

I knew then that I had made the wrong choice, that this bad man was not my grandfather and would never love me. But it was too late to go back.

2

The Village

When the logging truck dropped us off we moved into some kind of military truck, carrying soldiers. Sometimes we rode in horse-drawn carts. There were people everywhere. A momentous change had dragged practically everyone in Cambodia back on to the road. After four years of Khmer Rouge border attacks, the Communist government of Vietnam had invaded Cambodia in 1979. After the Vietnamese defeated the Khmer Rouge, they set up a new government, and from everywhere, starved and terrified people began moving back to their home villages. A year or so later, when my journey took place, the country was still swarming with movement.

I knew none of this at the time, of course, but I was mesmerised by the crowds. The roads. The motorcycles.

All the noise. The people looked beautiful, their skin so pale and their clothes ingenious. There were markets, with forks, bottles, string, shoes, matches, cigarettes, medicine, cosmetics, radios, guns – all things I had never seen. There was so much metal, and so much colour.

We were travelling south-east, across the border into Vietnam, though the concept of 'Vietnam' – or even 'Cambodia' – meant nothing at all to me then. Grandfather was delivering a load of sandalwood from the forest to a trader in Dalat, in the high plains of southern Vietnam, and I helped him carry it. After Dalat we travelled south, towards Saigon, and then began circling back.

One day I caught sight of a crowd of Vietnamese girls in their white tunics and trousers, like a huge flock of white birds. I was hypnotised. I suppose they were leaving school, but I had no idea what school was, nor any idea that I might go to one; I could see they were girls, but to me they looked more like angels.

Everywhere I went, I remember, I was horrified by the way people shouted at each other. Especially in Vietnam, they were also scornful of me, a dirty dark-skinned girl with no more brains than a lump of wood. They pushed me, yelled at me, insulted me.

I knew nothing, and I asked nothing. I just kept silent. Everything was unfamiliar, and dangerous. When Grandfather bought Vietnamese noodle soup I tried to eat the long slippery stuff with my hands, though the soup was boiling hot.

As we made our way back north, towards the Mekong river, the flat Cambodian countryside was unlike anything I had ever seen, flooded with rice-paddies in every direction. To me it looked empty, as empty as I felt. I had a mission in this hostile flatland – to find my parents – but I was no longer sure that I could.

Eventually the road disappeared into the swelling waters of the Mekong river. The rainy season was coming. We got on a large, two-storey ferry that was crammed with people and animals. We arrived in a village on the riverbank. There were wooden houses on stilts, about forty of them, and red dirt paths snaking around the fields and into the trees. This was Thloc Chhroy, the Deep Hole, so named because the banks of the Mekong are especially steep there.

Grandfather had a house in Thloc Chhroy, a little way from the river, made of woven palm leaves and palm trunks, with a bamboo floor. This village wasn't where he came from, and I don't know when or why he settled there. He had no wife or family and he spoke Cham, Khmer, Viet and Chinese. Nobody knew where he came from. Perhaps he too suffered during the terrible years of the Khmer Rouge regime.

Grandfather's house was small and ramshackle, half falling over with one room, a sleeping-pallet in the corner, and a charcoal brazier outside. It was my job to clean it, to cook, to fetch water from the river and to wash the clothes. He beat some Cham words into me, enough so that I understood what he said.

I was his domestic servant. Such things are common in Cambodia. It didn't matter if Grandfather bought me from Taman or not. Now that I was there, and he fed me and gave me lodging, I had to serve him and owed him obedience.

Pretty quickly, I learned enough Khmer to understand the insults the villagers called out to me, the only Phnong in the village. I was fatherless, black and ugly. Like most Khmer, the people in Thloc Chhroy see us Phnong as barbarians and uncontrollably violent – some even say we are cannibals. Of course, this is completely untrue. The Phnong are in fact very honest people, true to their word and straight with each other, and peaceful – unless, of course, they are provoked by Khmer attacks. They also do not beat or otherwise ill-treat their children, which all the villagers in Thloc Chhroy seemed to do; this shocked me.

The Khmer may scorn us as cannibals, but we Phnong see them as treacherous, like serpents that never move straight and will hurt you even if they have no need to eat.

Even though he was a Muslim, Grandfather gambled frequently. He would take his small wooden chess set wherever he went. He smoked cheroots of rolled-up tobacco leaves and drank rice alcohol every night. When he didn't have enough money for drink his eyes would grow hard. He would make me kneel and beat me with a long, hard bamboo that cut into my flesh and made me bleed with every blow.

I learned fear, and obedience. Grandfather made me work for other people to earn him money. Every morning I had to fetch water from the river for several villagers. At first it was almost impossible to climb up the steep riverbanks with the heavy buckets balanced on a stick across my shoulders. I would slip and fall, the zinc buckets cutting into the backs of my legs. Sometimes the cuts became so infected I could hardly walk.

In the evening I used stones to grind rice into flour before I could make it into noodles for dinner. That's how it was, in those days. If you had enough rice to eat, you were rich. We often didn't. When that happened, Grandfather and I would root in the food that the other villagers had thrown out for their pigs.

Grandfather often rented out my labour during the day. I worked in the rice-paddies, near the river. In the dry season we rebuilt the small clay walls that kept the water in, and when the river began to rise, we planted seedlings.

Sometimes men and boys would appear from the forest and help us pick the rice. They were Khmer Rouge fighters. In those days there were still large groups of soldiers in the countryside. There was a new, Vietnamese-backed government in power now, but the Khmer Rouge didn't melt away into thin air. Instead, Pol Pot's army retreated into hiding.

For a long time, there were a lot of skirmishes in the countryside between the Vietnamese-backed government army and the Khmer Rouge fighters. In Thloc Chhroy we often heard outbursts of gunfire and exploding land-mines, and many times soldiers or Khmer Rouge fighters came running through the village.

When this happened, the villagers always ran back indoors. They were terrified. It was important not to see, not to hear, not to know anything about what was happening.

One time a boy who often worked in the fields with me – he wasn't right in the head – went looking for a buffalo at nightfall, even though there had been a lot of shooting. We found his body the next morning. His head had been cut off, and it had rolled into the scrub along-side the path.

I don't know which side was responsible – the Khmer Rouge or the government – and I'm sure I didn't really understand the difference. In those days, nobody talked in Cambodia. Nobody wanted to explain the nightly murder and starvation and death camps of the four years they had just lived through under the Khmer Rouge, or that now we were living under Vietnamese occupation. They never talked about the Pol Pot time, the years of starvation and murder. It was as if they had blanked it out.

People learned from those years that they couldn't trust anyone; friends, neighbours, not even their own family. The more you let people know about yourself – the more you speak – the more you expose yourself to danger. This is a very Cambodian attitude to life.

So I never saw parents explaining things to their children. They told them what work to do, and they beat them. Many children were beaten every day, as I was, and some of them were much younger than me. It's mostly women, in these cases, who do the beating. Men usually hit more rarely, but when they do, it's more dangerous because they're so much stronger.

I dreamed of killing Grandfather, but it never occurred to me to slip away and try to make my way back home to the forest. That part of my life was gone for ever: somehow it didn't seem possible to me to make my way back. Now that I had discovered his true nature, I hated him. But I owed this man, even though he starved and hurt me, because I belonged to him. He accused me of bringing him bad luck. Since I'd been with him, he said, everything was going wrong with his business, and it was my fault.

Sometimes Grandfather would leave on long trips and I would breathe a sigh of relief. But most of the time he didn't work – he would sit at home, or gamble, and leave it to me to bring in the money. If I washed the dishes before I went to get fresh water he beat me because there was no water to drink, and if I went to get fresh water before I did the dishes he beat me because the dishes weren't done. Sometimes I cried, but I grew accustomed to neutralising my emotions. Who could I count on? People seemed to think it was normal that I should be beaten by one person or another, since I was this small black 'savage', the lowest person in the village.

Most of the people I fetched water for never had a kind word for me. They were only angry when I came late, or if the water had spilled a little. But one elderly woman who lived alone was good to me. She used to fuss over my cut feet. One day she gave me a pair of blue rubber flip-flops – my first shoes. They rubbed between my toes and they were very worn: the soles had huge holes and were so thin that thorns could pierce my feet through them. But they were shoes and, to me, that was really something.

From time to time I'd chat with her. I asked her why Cambodians were so horrible to the 'black savages', why they accused us of being cannibals. While I was living with those supposed savages no one had ever beaten me, but in Thloc Chhroy the villagers beat their children for the most trivial things. So who were the savages?

I remember the misery I felt during that first dry season in Thloc Chhroy. Huge piles of rice stalks had been piled into haystacks and I began to burrow holes into them, making nests in which I could hide from Grandfather. I began sleeping there sometimes. It was dark and hidden, safe.

After a few months I found another place in which I could take refuge. A younger boy who worked with me in the rice fields used to go and eat at the schoolteacher's house, and he took me along too. Mam Khon, the village schoolteacher, was poor, but he and his wife looked after children. They had six of their own, but they also fed a number of children who attended school but lived too far away to return to their homes every day. There were often twenty or more children in the house. It was a small house on stilts, with just one room – everyone slept on the floor, and in the dry season the boys slept downstairs, on the bare earth, on beds laid out underneath the house.

Mam Khon's wife, Pen Navy, made cakes that she used to sell. Sometimes she would give me one. I began helping her with the cooking, and eating over there sometimes. She fed us all, though the family was so poor it often wasn't even rice, just rice soup.

She was kind, but in manner Pen Navy was a stern woman, rough and authoritarian. She was half-Chinese and had very pale skin – I thought she was beautiful. One afternoon while we were working she asked me why I didn't go to school.

The village school was an open-air classroom with a thatched roof for shelter from the rain; Mam Khon and another teacher had started it up again after the Khmer Rouge regime fell. There was a uniform – dark blue skirt and white shirt – and crowds of laughing children. Of course, I longed to go there, but I didn't think Grandfather would ever let me, and I told her this. I called her 'Aunty', as a sign of respect. For a while we left it at that. It was clear to us both that Grandfather had the right to stop me going if he wanted to.

Mam Khon himself hovered over the household like an apparition – he was a gentle, good man, but he rarely spoke. One day he found me crying because the other children had insulted me. He bent down – he was a tall man, with a strong face and clear, dark eyes – and took my face in his. 'You're not a savage,' he said. 'You're the daughter of my brother. My brother left to go to Mondulkiri with a woman and had a child there, and now I have found that child – it's you.'

I had no idea whether or not I should believe him. But Mam Khon told me he would register me for school, and he said he would sort this out with Grandfather. And Grandfather finally agreed that I could go to school so long as it didn't cost him anything. School itself was free in those days, because we were living under Communism, so what he meant by that was that I must still work for him and bring him money.

School was from 7 a.m. until 11 a.m., but if I got up long before dawn to fetch the water and bring home the money, I'd be able to wash and dress in time to leave for school. But then Mam Khon's colleague, Mr Chai, said I couldn't register for first grade – I was already over ten and therefore far too old.

Mam Khon told him a story to appease him. 'She's my daughter,' he said. 'I lost her in the Troubles, but now I've found her. She's mine.' This was how I got my name: Mam Somaly. Mam, like him. And Somaly, which he had chosen for me. I liked it.

I was always careful to wash and care for my school uniform – I was so proud of it. The skirt and shirt were hand-me-downs, from Mam Khon's daughters, but to me they were beautiful. At last, I felt I was like everyone else. But the others didn't feel the same way. The village children called me '*Khmao*', which is like 'nigger'.

The darker you were, the dumber – this was an established fact. But I found it wasn't true. I studied and learned quickly and well. I learned to read and write Khmer, as well as mathematics.

There was no school in the afternoon, but we often had to do physical work there: every school was supposed to have a productive component, a vegetable garden or rice-field. We planted jackfruit trees and coconut palms. I remember when we had to dig a huge pit in the schoolyard for a duckpond: it was hard, dirty work, and also fun.

Sometimes in the afternoons we did military training in the neighbouring field. The soldiers taught us to clean and handle rifles, to shoot, and to throw a hand-grenade. We learned how to dig a deep pit with sharp spikes sticking up in the bottom of it, to capture men, and to cover it with large dry leaves. There was still a war going on in the countryside.

There were accidents. Sometimes during military training children were wounded. Once a hand grenade blew off a boy's foot. They took him away, but he died. This was sad but didn't seem to affect people greatly. Death was random, normal – it was too routine to care much about one kid.

I remember the time the teacher asked us to list all the bad things that had happened to us under the Khmer Rouge. I had been living in the forest with the Phnong – nothing had happened to me under Pol Pot, so I gave back my paper blank. This teacher was Mam Khon's colleague, Mr Chai, a dark-skinned man, pinched and dry. To punish me, he made me kneel for an hour in the sun on thorny, hardened skins of dried jackfruit. My knees bled.

But other than that there were no real punishments in school – I was never tied down and lashed, as Grandfather used to do with me when he was drunk and out of money.

When we did military training I always took the role of the Khmer Rouge, because I wanted everyone to be frightened of me. I hated everyone – not just the children in my class, but all Khmer. I didn't hate the Khmer Rouge fighters who sometimes melted out of the forest to help us with the harvest, and I didn't hate the government soldiers who taught us either. Occasionally the soldiers would give us things to eat – their rations allowed for milk and sugar. There were times I would have sold my soul for a glass of milk.

After about a year it got better. I had a new best friend, Pana, a boy who worked in the fields too, who lived in a nearby village. We used to walk home together, though his walk was longer than mine. One day I had just arrived at Mam Khon's house when we all heard a huge explosion from the direction he had taken. Mam Khon told me to take his bicycle and I rode to Pana's house on it, still too small to reach the saddle. He had exploded. A rocket-propelled grenade had hit him. A soldier some distance away had apparently banged his RPG down and it had gone off. Pana's hand was in a tree, his arm was somewhere else – there was no body left, but I helped find all the pieces. Afterwards I had nightmares about it. I went to the pagoda sometimes to pray for him. It was a long time before the nightmares went away.

Pana was my first friend, and he was dead. I thought maybe I really did bring misfortune, just like Grandfather said.

In my second year in school, I came top of the class. In those days, under Communism, the best students were given awards that were meaningful – bolts of cloth, and milk and rice. That year I received two bolts of cotton, blue and pink. I took them over to Mam Khon's house and his wife helped me cut out and sew a pink shirt with a heart-shaped pocket, and a blue skirt. They were my most precious possessions, the first new clothes I had ever had. I kept that blouse until I was in my twenties and it burned with Mam Khon's entire house in a fire.

I began, shyly, to call Mam Khon 'Father' a few months after he first took me to the school. It doesn't sound so unusual in Khmer. It's a tone of closeness and respect, but other children called him '*Pok*' too. He was such a good man. He used to take me out fishing with him. He could never have survived on his minuscule salary as a schoolteacher, but he had a small, low rowing boat we used to take up the Mekong in the evenings, trailing our nets along bamboo poles at different levels to catch various kinds of fish.

At around three in the morning we would tie up in mid-river with other fishing boats – once you were away from the village it was much too dangerous to ever sleep on the banks. Then, at dawn, we would make our way back and sell our fish on the banks. We gave the rest of the catch to his wife and daughters to ferment and make into *prahoc* sauce, or simply to dry. That way we could always trade dried fish for rice when the wet season came and fishing was difficult. There wasn't much money in those days, and we traded for everything.

We never talked much -- Father was a silent person. But we grew closer, spending time alone together on the river. He taught me how to mend nets and throw them flat and wide. I loved to be out on the Mekong, far from other people, even though I knew it wasn't particularly normal for a girl to be doing this work. Father's daughters never liked to fish: I suppose they thought it was disgusting, or maybe they were worried about keeping their pale skin out of the sun and the wind.

I tried to work hard for Father's family so they would let me stay there as much as possible. Of Father's six children, the two eldest were both girls. Soechenda was the eldest, about fourteen, and Sophanna was two years older than me, but I felt they were so far ahead – in school, in life, in everything. They were pale and beautiful, and they cooked and washed and studied during the day in the house with their mother. They had time for study and were allowed to use an oil lamp to study by. This seemed miraculous – when I studied, it was by moonlight.

Soechenda and Sophanna and the younger children were not overjoyed to have me as their new sister – for now I took to calling them 'Sister', and their mother, 'Mother', too. Still, they were not horrible about it. Even Sophanna, the little princess of them all – the prettiest and the palest-skinned – could be very nice.

This was a real Cambodian family, by which I mean people never spoke about personal matters. It was not only inappropriate, but would give other people a hold on you. One should never give anything of oneself away, either in public or in private. Somebody who understands you can use your words to mock you, or betray you. Confiding means you are weak. Anything you say may one day be used against you. Better to hide what you think and feel.

There was a fortune-teller in the village, an old woman who lived near the river in a hut even more derelict than Grandfather's. Everyone respected her and went to her for advice. I must have been about twelve years old when Mam Khon's wife took us all there one day. I think she really meant to ask about her daughters' wedding prospects, which we all assumed were good – they were both so pretty and white – but the fortune-teller said Sophanna would have an unlucky life with a lot of misfortune. Then she looked at me and said, 'But the black one – she will have the three flags' – power, honour, and money. 'She will travel in a plane and she will be a leader in the family. She will help you.'

The other children hooted with mirth. Sophanna laughed the loudest – 'You'll have children so dark you won't be able to see them at night,' she told me. It was good-humoured; I joined in the laughing. It just didn't seem possible that this would be my destiny.

Sophanna didn't believe I was her sister in a real, biological sense, or even her half-sister, and neither, to be honest, did I. I also wasn't sure about the story that these were my cousins. Another time Father found me crying I asked him about it, and he told me he really was the older brother of my father. He said his brother had left, and married a Phnong woman, and had a child, and that this man – his brother, my father – had a bad temper just like me. He held a mirror up and pointed to his eyes and mine, his forehead and said, 'We are the same.'

Another time he told me, 'Your uncle, your father, it doesn't matter – the important thing is that we are together.' I suspect he knows what really happened to my parents, but he has never talked to me about it. Finally, I have listened to his advice: I no longer ask.

My breasts were growing, and Grandfather began touching them. He would roll heavily across the sleeping pallet at night and I would feel his hands on me. When he did this, I ran. I was fast – even today, people in the village remember me running. I would run down to the river in the dark and sleep there, on the banks, where we kept the fishing boats. The reflection of the moon in the water calmed me, and I would curl into the roots of a tree or crawl into Father's boat and sleep on the nets. I continued to do my water duty and leave Grandfather the money that I'd earned, but I left as soon as possible, and during the day I tried always to be at school or at Father's house.

One evening, a couple of months after we went to the fortune-teller, Grandfather asked me to get oil for the lamp from the Chinese merchant where we bought our goods. The request sounded innocent enough – there was no electricity, so we used an oil lamp. I often bought things from the Chinese merchant – he traded in rice and loaned people money at high interest, and he and his wife were respected in the village. Sometimes they gave me sweets or cakes.

But that day the merchant's wife wasn't there. The merchant had me follow him to the storeroom to offer me a cake. Then he threw me down on a pile of rice sacks and held me down. He hit me hard and raped me. I didn't know what he had done but it felt as though he had cut me in between my legs.

And then he threatened me: 'If you tell anyone, I'll cut your throat. Your grandfather owes me a lot of money. If you talk to him about it, he will beat you. So shut it.' He held out some striped candy.

I didn't take it. I refused and ran. I was bleeding. I felt a horrible shame. I didn't understand what had happened, but I went to the riverbank. I told the tree about my pain and my disgust at these evil people, especially the Chinese man who had insulted and hurt me.

I tried to throw myself into the Mekong that night, at a place where the riverbank is very steep. I went under. But I couldn't help swimming – it seemed that I couldn't make myself die. I washed up along the muddy bank a little further downstream.

When I got back to Grandfather's, he beat me. He said it was because I was late. He didn't even ask what had happened to the oil I was supposed to bring. But I realised somehow that he knew what had happened to me, and that he had sent me to the merchant that night on purpose.

I went back to the fortune-teller and I shouted at her. I told her she was talking nonsense, that she was an old madwoman who told lies.

Nowadays I understand that Grandfather owed that Chinese merchant money, and that he sold him my virginity to pay his debt. In Cambodia, many men believe a virgin will keep you strong and imbue you with fresh strength: today it is widely held that raping a virgin will also cure you of Aids. I can see now that what the Chinese man did to me was rape, but at the time I had no words for it – I didn't know about penises; I thought he used a knife.

I also knew that I had to keep quiet, that this was something I could never talk about. Not only because of the fear the Chinese merchant had filled me with, but also because it had something to do with things that were unspeakable in a Khmer family. Until today, I've never told my adoptive father about the rape. I felt good in that family, and I knew that if I opened my mouth I'd be beaten, because Cambodian people don't talk about such things. It would only shame me and the people who heard me.

I learned to shut down all my feelings so that none of it mattered – so that it never even happened. Pain is temporary. It goes away if you let your brain go numb.

After that night, I no longer wanted to speak. I no

longer wanted to understand Khmer. I closed myself up in silence and lived like a mute. The next time Grandfather asked me to go and get oil for the lamp, I refused and he beat me. Then he went to get some of those red ants that sting so viciously it hurts for weeks.

I tried never to sleep at Grandfather's house. But I always had to go back every morning and evening, to bring him money and cook his meal. Today of course I would leave – today, I would probably kill him – but then, as a child, I just never thought of leaving. Maybe I was stupid, but there seemed to be nowhere I could go. I couldn't just settle in as part of Father's family – that would create conflict between my adoptive father and Grandfather, and Father hated conflict of any kind, with anyone.

So I continued to do chores for other families after school and to take the money to Grandfather. One day when I was doing the dishes for an old woman, I was startled and I dropped a glass, which broke. The old woman picked up a cane and started to beat me like a fury. My back was all bloody. At school I couldn't sit down, I was so cut up. I ran a high fever. My adoptive parents took care of me. They rubbed *moxa* on me – a traditional paste of herbs, which stings. It hurt so much I was crying. Father explained to me that in life one has to bear suffering. No matter how much it hurts, it is best to stay quiet.

He always used to say, 'If you want to stay alive, grow a *dam kor* tree in front of your house.' The *dam kor* is the silk cotton tree, but the same word, *kor,* also means mute. To survive, you must be silent.

When the dry season came, Father began letting me and one of his young sons, Sothea, take out the fishing boat by ourselves. Sothea was about four or five years old, a quiet kid with hair that spiked right out of his head and huge, perpetually astonished eyes. I was about twelve, but I liked having him around. Sometimes we went out in the evening and slept with the fishing families on the red earth down by the boats. Sothea helped me build a shelter of palm-leaves and bamboo by the riverbank where I could sleep – it was just four bamboo poles and dried palm leaves for a roof. I made a floor out of dried rice stalks from the fields and I slept there.

It wasn't dangerous. A lot of people lived by the river. If I went out fishing at night I would give a handful of rice to someone who was staying by the bank. When I came back from the river my rice would be cooked and we could share a fish. Every morning I would give my catch to Father and we would sell some, and if I had enough money to give to Grandfather I could go to school that day.

In the wet season, when the Mekong swelled and flooded the banks, a lot of wood would come down the river. We would go out in boats to grab it and haul it in. We could dry it, to burn in the fire. Sometimes we sold it, or traded it for rice, but mostly we kept it for Father's family.

At school, Mr Chai began selecting children to train

for a show of traditional Cambodian dance. Everyone was astonished when he picked me. He explained that at night, make-up would show up better on my skin than on the paler girls. Also, I had very long hair, unlike most of the other girls: under the Khmer Rouge, everyone's hair had to be short.

Mr Chai trained us in the precise gestures of the *apsaras*, to curve our fingertips and hold our necks stiffly, like cranes. I didn't care much for the music or the dance, but people thought I was pretty, and I liked their admiration and surprise.

We still lived very collectively in those days. It wasn't like today, when individual families keep more to themselves, especially in cities. Cambodia was a Communist country. Every village was organised into groups called *krom samaki* – eight or ten families who would plant the rice together and share the labour of the village's buffaloes. After the harvest the group leader would share it out; every family would receive perhaps fifty kilos of rice for the year.

I look back, now, at those days and I think it was the best system for Cambodia. School was free and it gave children a way out of poverty – not like today, when parents must pay huge sums of money for education and every diploma is for sale. Hospitals were few and poorly equipped then, but they were practically free. Nowadays you could be dying, but if you can't pay they won't look after you.

Communism wasn't like life under the Khmer Rouge. People were no longer frightened. They no longer had to

obey the orders of murderous young children who had
been indoctrinated by the government. And so now they
began to relax into the old ways. The elderly ordered the
young about instead of the other way round. Women no
longer called their husband 'comrade', as they had to
under the Khmer Rouge, but 'older brother' or 'uncle',
and now they had to behave with the proper submission
and respect.

Like all the girls at Father's house, I had to learn to
chant the *chbap srey*, the code of good behaviour for
Cambodian maidens. It was part of the school curricu-
lum – part of the government's desire to erase what the
Khmer Rouge had done and go back to the old culture.
All the girls in school had to learn to chant it, but
Mam Khon wanted us to be word-perfect.

Ideally, in Cambodia a woman walks so quietly you
can't hear her footsteps. She smiles without showing her
teeth and laughs softly. She never looks directly into the
eyes of any man. A woman must not talk back to her
husband. She must not turn her back to him in bed. She
must bow before she touches his head, and if she walks
over his legs she will become ill. In Cambodia, you must
respect and care for your parents, and your husband is
your master – he is second only to your father.

I was obedient, but I was not gentle. I seethed. I
remember one afternoon when I was out fishing with
Sothea. The two of us were on the riverbank when we
caught sight of some rich people – people from Phnom
Penh, the capital. To me they looked like gods, especially the woman – slender and pale, with clothes that

31

looked new and shoes with pointy toes. She talked softly and almost glided. She was so pretty; I was overcome with admiration.

I said to Sothea, 'Maybe one day we'll be rich like them.' He stood up and waved his arms, he was so excited. Sothea said, 'We must really believe that – we *will* be rich like them. We must work hard at school and we can do it!' He told me he wanted to become a trader. I told him, 'If I get married one day I want to marry a rich man – a soldier, so he can kill Grandfather.'

3

'This is Your Husband'

Soechenda, Mam Khon's eldest daughter, was due to
pass her school leaving certificate, a real achievement in
our village. She was seventeen, and a rough equivalent
would be the end of GCSEs. (I, aged fourteen, had still
not quite finished primary school.) There was great
excitement in the family, because if Soechenda passed
she could go on to further studies, still a rare thing for a
village girl.

It was a national examination, and it took place in
Kampong Cham, the provincial capital, which was
about three hours on a bicycle from Thloc Chhroy. It
was decided that we would all go there with Mother,
and spend the night on the way at the house of one of
Mother's aunts.

That night, at Grandmother's house, Sophanna woke me up to urge me to listen, because downstairs the old woman and Mother were talking. They were saying how lucky Mother had been to find a good man. We heard that, when she was young, Mother's stepmother had taken her to another town – with or without her father's knowledge – and had sold her into a brothel. She had suffered a great deal. Father was a poor man, and young, but he loved her, and after he got his school diploma he went to find her in the brothel and he bought her out.

All this had happened long before the Khmer Rouge, in the impenetrable time when Father and Mother were young. I suppose it was probably the 1950s. Sophanna and I were overwhelmed by this revelation, and we cried together. Mother had never told us anything about her past. She simply couldn't, and she still can't. We have never discussed it.

I think selling women into prostitution has always existed in Cambodia. People get into debt – it's easy, when the interest is 10 per cent or more (much more) a month. By working in a brothel where the moneylender has an arrangement, a daughter acts as collateral and repays the loan. Expenses, such as food, clothes, medicine and make-up, are extracted from her account, of course, and the parents can contract more debts, too.

In other cases the parents sell their daughters outright to the brothel. It's like they transfer their ownership of her. A twelve-year-old girl might bring in fifty or a hundred US dollars for her family, or more if she has canny parents and very pale skin. The brothel has the right to sell her on. Other families just tell the girls to do it, and they obey. The family goes to the brothel every month or so to pick up her earnings. Daughters have a duty to obey their parents and provide for them.

I know this is hard to imagine. But after all these years, I can truly say that I think that for many parents, feelings have nothing to do with it. Their children are money on legs, an asset, a kind of domestic livestock.

About a month after we returned from that trip to Kampong Cham, Grandfather caught hold of my arm one morning when I was dropping off his money. He told me, 'Prepare your things and come to the house tonight.' I did what he said – it never occurred to me to disobey him outright. That evening, when I went back to his house, there was a man there, and Grandfather told me, 'This is your husband.'

I didn't think anything. I had long before made myself numb – it was rare for me to have emotions about anything that happened to me, in those days. Girls respect their elders, and I owed Grandfather obedience. This was just one more event in my life, after a lot of other events. It's possible that I felt a little relieved: perhaps I would be leaving Grandfather's house. But I didn't want to leave with *this* man. I knew I was only exchanging one master for another.

We went to the temple – it was a wooden hut that the villagers had constructed in the grounds of the old Buddhist pagoda, which the Khmer Rouge had destroyed.

There was a priest, but we had no ceremony to speak of. Usually there is a marriage ceremony and a big party, but it was just like Grandfather not to want to spend money on me. I wore my school skirt. We made offerings to the spirits at the temple, to respectfully request that they leave us alone: in Cambodia, you must constantly propitiate the spirits of the dead or they will come to your house and cause you harm. The priest said, 'You're married,' and that was that.

My new husband was older than me. I was about fourteen and he must have been in his mid-twenties. He was a soldier. Tall, dark-skinned, curly hair, white teeth. Quite nice-looking, and very violent. I hate to think about that man. Grandfather owed him money – he told me that later. My husband's name was Than, but I always called him *'pou'* – 'uncle' – as a mark of submission and deference.

The first night of my marriage I slept at Grandfather's house and my husband slept elsewhere. The next day we travelled, with Grandfather, to Chup, where my husband was stationed. It was a trip of about 120 kilometres, and it took from dawn till late at night: first the boat to Kampong Cham and then a truck.

Before we left I went to Mam Khon's house. I told Mother that Grandfather had married me to a man. She told me, 'Maybe it is for the best. You must leave with him, and perhaps it will be better with him than with your grandfather.' She and Father must have suspected how often I was beaten, though we never talked about it.

*

36

My husband's house was a small shack built by the army amid the rubber plantations. It was one empty room, stained by red dirt and empty except for a cooking fire and a bamboo sleeping platform.

I hate marriage. It puts women in prison. On her wedding day the girl obeys her parents, and when the ceremony is over she is raped. What does a young girl in Cambodia know about sex? Nothing. I had already had sex, of a kind, but even so I knew nothing about it. I didn't know what the Chinese merchant had put inside me – only that it hurt – and I had no idea that this was what happened in marriage.

I don't think I was unusual in my ignorance. One time, at school, when we were in military training, a boy stepped over a girl's back and she cried, because she thought that now she was pregnant. We were all like that. People told their daughters you got pregnant if you touched a boy's hand.

My husband raped me on that platform that first night, several times, and when I resisted him he hit me. He grabbed my hair and smacked my head on the wall, and then he slapped me hard so I would fall down on the bed.

When it was morning I had to get up and make food. There was no explanation – no mercy, or shame, ever. We hardly ever spoke to each other, in any case.

I saw other people only when I walked into the village to buy food. I cooked grasshoppers, vegetables, dried fish – he ate what I served him. If he didn't like it he hit me.

That man – my husband – beat me often. Sometimes with the butt of his rifle on my back, smashing it down with both his hands, and sometimes with his hands. With his fingernails, which he kept long and pointed, he gashed a deep scar into my cheek. He did it because I didn't smile, because I wasn't welcoming, because I was ugly and I had a death's head – that's what he called me.

He was very violent. Many soldiers are. When he was angry I would try to breathe as softly as possible, so as not to be noticed, because anything could set him off. Sometimes he shot at me, with his military rifle, to frighten me. At first it worked – it frightened me a lot – but I grew used to it. Inside, I felt that I was dead. When he raped me I would try to disappear.

This was my life – another kind of domestic slavery. I never spoke to anyone about it. There were houses around us, with other soldiers and other soldier's wives in them, but you don't talk about such things. Cambodians have a saying: you must not let the fire that is outside come inside your house and the hearth fire must not be allowed outside. You don't talk about what happens in your house. Probably the other wives were beaten too: the frequency varies, but in my country the beating is normal.

My husband was often gone, fighting the Khmer Rouge. The government couldn't afford to lose control of the rubber plantations, and the region was crawling with soldiers. When he left, I would quickly run out of money for food, with no idea of when he'd come back. Going back to Thloc Chhroy simply wasn't an option: Grandfather would only beat me, and I knew my husband would too, when he came back.

Chup was separated into two parts – the village itself, and then, near the rubber plantations, where I lived, the clinic and the military grounds. The clinic was always full of wounded soldiers, and people from the village were also brought there when landmines exploded as they worked in the fields, blowing off their legs or hands. There were landmines everywhere. The Khmer Rouge laid mines, and the government soldiers laid them to stop the Khmer Rouge from moving around the plantations – maybe there was even unexploded ordnance from the American bombing of Cambodia at the end of the Vietnam war.

Nobody wanted to work at the clinic, especially at night, even though you were paid thirteen kilos of rice every month. Nobody wanted to handle body parts and dead people. But all I wanted was to work – I wasn't frightened of the dead. A dead body was like my body, no difference at all. Once or twice, though, I did step on a severed leg or arm in the dark – that, I admit, was horrible.

Sometimes, when landmine victims came in, all we could do was amputate. If there was no anaesthetic, which was often, we tied the person down. There were doctors at the clinic, but they weren't proper doctors – they were just medics who had learned their job under the Khmer Rouge. If they weren't there we nurses had to carry out the operations ourselves. Only one of us had any medical training at all: our chief nurse had done a course in Phnom Penh for a few months.

We learned by trial and error – mainly error. When our stocks of medication ran low we diluted it. People died of gangrene, of malaria, or lack of blood. The worst, to me, were the women who died in childbirth. There I felt real pity. One woman, who was expecting twins, suffered for hours. We didn't know how to perform a Caesarean. I was so tired that after she died I fell asleep on the spot, on the floor right next to her body.

Washing hands was not a habit: we often ran out of soap. So many people perished in pain. Obviously, all these years later, I can see that what we did to the patients at that time was awful. But we were poor and ignorant. It was the situation that was terrible.

About six months after I was married I got my period for the first time. I was fifteen, and I thought perhaps a leech from the lake had hurt me: I had no idea why I should bleed. I stayed at home all day – my husband was away fighting. When I went back to work at the clinic I told my colleague Pouv. Then the chief nurse arrived, and she was angry with me. She asked me for my excuse, and when I told her my secret place was bleeding – that is what we say – she was still angry, but she explained. She took me to the cupboard where she kept clean cloth, for bandages, and she said it was what happened to women.

Pouv hadn't had her periods yet either. She was dark-skinned and her face wasn't pretty; none of the other nurses liked her, but I did. She was about fifteen too. Pouv was an orphan like me – she lived with her uncle, who beat her. She told me he raped her, too. I never told her about my husband, but that was when I realised that I wasn't alone – that when my husband hurt me between my legs, this too was what happened to other women.

The doctors at that clinic preyed on us – especially the pretty white-skinned ones, or the orphans who had nobody to protect them. There was nothing we could do but submit. At first I was spared, because I was ugly and married. But it didn't last for ever.

The doctor who did it to me told me afterwards, 'You're so ugly you're lucky I'm doing this.' The rape wasn't as bad as the words. I felt like garbage, like I was nothing, and also I was frightened of my husband. In Cambodia a woman must not have sex with another man, and if it does happen she should kill herself.

I tried. I swallowed a lot of Russian Yazipam sleeping drops from the clinic. The next day I woke up stunned and bleary, and when I went back to work a day later the chief nurse told me off.

Grandfather appeared again. He needed money. And he had a letter for me: an invitation. Sophanna was to be married, and she asked me to come, to be her bridesmaid. After Grandfather left I got permission from the clinic to go. I paid a man to take me there, riding on the back of his bicycle. I arrived the night before the wedding, and when I got to the house Sophanna was getting ready.

I asked her, 'Who is your husband?' She didn't know. She waved her hand at a clump of young men outside the house, watching the preparations. 'Maybe one of them,' she said. I asked her, 'And are you glad?'

There was going to be a priest, several dresses to change into, make-up, cakes, a ceremony, but she looked at me emptily. I was fifteen, so Sophanna must have been eighteen by then. I thought she was very lucky to have been allowed to wait so long, though I knew some of the other villagers called Father's household 'the old virgins'.

Father was a teacher, an intellectual, and Mother was schooled too. They had not forced Sophanna. Mother asked her, 'Do you want to marry?' and Sophanna answered, 'As you wish,' because that is what good girls do. That seemed normal to her, and it did to me as well.

She didn't ask me about sex, and I didn't tell her. Such things are never said. But I heard Mother say, 'On the first night, you sleep facing your husband. If you turn your back on him that means you'll divorce. And you let him do what he wants.' I realised that this always happened in marriage – that this was what marriage was about.

Grandfather wasn't in the village and it was decided that I would stay at Father's house that night. Sophanna had made me a dress. I was so proud to be introduced as Sophanna's sister: the husband's family just assumed that meant these were my real father and mother, my real family. The husband was a boy of about eighteen, from a nearby village – he had been hiding from the government soldiers who had recently been coming around to conscript all the boys.

I returned to Chup. Shortly after, my husband went away again, but this time much further. The fighting was becoming intense along the Cambodian border with Thailand, at Kor 5. The Khmer Rouge forces were growing. They were now an army, based in Thailand. At the end of every year the Vietnamese forces that occupied Cambodia would go on the offensive and destroy the guerrilla bases there, but after the dry season, as the rains resumed, the Khmer Rouge would move back into the country. Now the government was building a huge wall of landmines and man-traps along the border, to stop the Khmer Rouge from coming across.

My husband left with his contingent for the border. The weeks went by: he didn't come back.

A month or so after he left, Grandfather turned up once more. The first time I gave him money and he went away. The second time I had no money to give him, so he beat me. It had been a long time since he'd done that. Then he told me, 'Prepare your bag. We're going to visit an aunty, in the city.'

4

Aunt Nop

The city meant going to the capital of Cambodia. In those days Phnom Penh was nothing like as prosperous or as wild as it is now. There was hardly any electricity. There were fewer vagrants in the streets. The buildings were wrecked and crumbling, the windows had no glass in them, and the roads were a jumble of stones, mud and rubbish. A decade after the Khmer Rouge emptied the cities and sent all their inhabitants to work camps, the roads and basic utilities had still not been repaired.

The country was still Communist. But there were already nightclubs with local music, bars and huge crowds of people. I was bewildered by all the noise – by all the streets and the buildings. I had never seen anywhere so wealthy and so crowded.

There were huge, cacophonous markets selling every-thing from cooking pots to car parts, with massive displays of food – fruit and vegetables that I couldn't even recognise, and what seemed like oceans of fish. There were crowds of motorcycles, too – more motor-cycles than I had ever imagined could exist – and black Russian bicycles, shiny and new.

Even girls rode bicycles here. I thought some of those people looked like they were living in heaven. But I didn't think that Grandfather was taking me to the city for any good reason. I knew nothing good could come from that man.

We arrived that first evening at around dusk. Aunt Nop lived in a small, dirty apartment in the narrow old streets around the central market. We walked upstairs in the gloom – it was on the second floor, and there was no electricity in the building. She eyed me sharply through the half-opened door.

Aunt Nop was about thirty-five, I suppose. She was a Muslim Cham like Grandfather, but she wore Western clothes and had her hair set in waves. She had a fat face and far too much make-up, smears of paint and eyebrows that she pencilled high up on her forehead. I thought she looked hideous, like a demon or some kind of evil spirit. Her face was expressionless: I never saw her smile.

While she and Grandfather talked I was told to wash. I went into a pitch-dark toilet. In the day that place was filthy and at night it was so small you felt it had become your coffin: I had to wash myself there often, in that little room.

That first night, Grandfather and Aunt Nop looked at me and talked some more. They sent me to the bedroom, where there was another girl a little older than me – perhaps seventeen or eighteen. She had almond eyes, like a Chinese, but dark skin. She didn't say anything, and neither did I.

Then Grandfather left. I saw Aunt Nop give him money before he went. He told me, 'Do what Aunty tells you. I'll be back.'

Aunt Nop lived with another woman her age and the woman's daughter, who was the girl in the bedroom. Her name was Mom. After Grandfather left, the women told me to sit still while Mom put make-up on me, and they gave me a dress and shoes – they said we were going out.

When we left the apartment it was already dark and I stumbled on the rubbish in the street. They took me to a long, filthy, pitch-black corridor between two street-front shop-houses. It led back into a dark courtyard and a warren of other alleyways. We went into a door-way and up a derelict flight of stairs. There was no banister left on the stairs – I suppose somebody had stolen it.

On the first floor there was a kind of apartment. There weren't any walls or floors to divide this place from the stairwell – it was just a bare concrete floor and you saw the beds and the blackened cooking fire as you walked up. There were many beds – rotting pallets made of woven grass. The place was filthy.

46

I am writing about this place because I never want to
have to talk about it again. I never want to have to
remember this another time. It makes me vomit.

The woman in charge of this place was Aunt Peuve.
She was a small woman, rather plump – plump for those
days, anyway – with a mole on her lower lip and her
hair in a bun.

A man arrived and I watched as he talked to Aunt Peuve.
She signalled to Mom, and before she got up Mom said,
'You'd better know what this is. It's a brothel. Do what
they say or they'll hit you.' Then she left and another
man came in and Aunt Peuve told him, 'She is a new
chicken, fresh from the country.'

In the corner, nearest the wall, there was a bed walled
off with a partition of sarongs. He went in there. She
came to get me and when I said, 'No,' she hit me on the
head, and said, 'Yes or no, you will do it.'

Her husband, Li, wasn't there at the time, but the
guards were there.

I went into the room, and I felt frightened, as if I had
been locked in a place with a hungry wild animal. He
was tall, he wore a shirt, he was in his thirties – maybe
he was a policeman, or perhaps he worked in an office.
He said, 'Take off your clothes, don't fight me. I don't
want to have to hurt you.'

I was from the country – in Thloc Chhroy nobody
ever took off all their clothes at once. They bathed
wearing clothes and changed clothes under a sarong.
I couldn't do a thing like that, in front of a stranger. I

fought him. He raped me but it wasn't easy, because I resisted.

So he did it again, to teach me another lesson. I was bleeding from the nose and mouth when he'd finished, and felt dirty: blood and sperm everywhere. It was morning, and when he left he said, 'I'll see you tonight.'

We went back to Aunt Nop's apartment and washed and slept. I felt a black, dark anger at Grandfather, at what he had done to me. In the evening it was time to put on make-up and go out again. When we got to Aunt Peuve's, she said, 'Don't do that again. I gave you to that man because he is so kind, and I knew he wouldn't hurt you as some of the others would have done.'

The next man had a beard, I remember; he was fat and he hit me with his belt buckle. He called Li. He was angry. Aunt Peuve's husband, Li, was an unbelievably violent man – he was an ex-soldier, and his foot had been blown off, so he walked with a crutch. He smashed the crutch on me and raped me that night, and afterwards so did his two guards. There was a Khmer guard with a puffy face like an alcoholic, and a hard-faced Chinese, whose body was horrible, thin and coiled with muscles. I hated that man. There was so much violence in him.

Cambodians are violent – they can beat you to death. Don't give any credence to those myths about the gentle Khmer smile. Men in Cambodia can seem gentle but when they're angry they can kill you with their bare fists.

Afterwards they took me down to the cellar. They

kept animals there, snakes and scorpions. They kept them to frighten us with – they weren't meant to kill us. It was a small room, totally dark, and it stank of sewage. They tied me up and before they left me there they dumped the snakes on me.

That was the punishment room. I was often taken there, because I'm difficult. The clients used to say I was ugly, or that I looked meanly at them – they often complained about me. The other girls said people had died there, and they were terrified just to be taken down the stairs because of their spirits. But I wasn't frightened of ghosts. The dead don't scare me. I cried, but it was because I had no parents, because I was helpless, because I had been raped and beaten, and I was hungry and exhausted. I cried from emotion, not from pain – from frustration, because I couldn't kill them. Grandfather, the guards – even my parents, who had left me to this. I missed my mother's love, and hated her for not being there. There was no love in my life.

I don't know when they let me out – a long time later. Perhaps the whole of the following day. By the time Mom walked me out my legs felt as though they weren't working properly. Aunt Nop was so angry with me she said, 'I'm not feeding you,' but I didn't want to eat anyway. It was Mom's mother who stopped Aunt Nop from beating me, because I'd had enough, she said, and it was true: I could see double. She made me clean all day and I wasn't allowed to sleep because I hadn't earned any money. Mom took pity on me and dabbed peroxide on my wounds. She knew what it was like.

After that I accepted the clients. There wasn't any choice.

During the day we lived at Aunt Nop's apartment. Later a third girl arrived. Aunt Nop specialised in new arrivals, girls straight from the countryside. She had the connections. But she rented rooms out to respectable people, and she didn't want clients in her apartment, so at night Aunt Nop took us to Aunt Peuve's brothel.

It was Aunt Nop who owned us, but Aunt Peuve who handled all the business. I suppose she gave her a cut. Aunt Nop and Aunt Peuve were *meebons*; women whose business is dealing in prostitutes. They looked after us, they fed us, they dressed us – though that was usually an expense we had to repay – and they lived with us. At night they rented us out.

Some prostitutes are sold to the *meebon* by their parents or relatives, or by their husbands. The price depends on their freshness and beauty, as well as the cleverness and connections of the seller. Today some girls are kidnapped into prostitution, but I don't think that used to happen so much when I was young. Most of the girls at Aunt Peuve's house were there as a kind of deposit, to pay back a debt. They were supposed to work until they paid back the money their families owed – or until the families took out new debts, extending their daughter's servitude.

Nobody wants you back after you've worked in a brothel. The word for prostitute in Cambodia is *srey kouc*, 'broken woman' – broken in a way that cannot be mended. You are for ever ruined and your existence itself shames the family. Nobody wants people to know they have a prostitute in their family.

The clients were horrible. To them we were produce. They would say, 'I paid a fortune and you're not even pretty,' and smack, hit you against the wall. Some of them liked hurting us and did it for sport. They were dirty. They stank. In my memory their dirtiness is the most repugnant thing. That, and the smell.

The soldiers and former soldiers were the most violent. They had a special kind of anger and ferocity. You felt it was uncontrollable and they might kill you at any time. I remember one man, who had been a soldier with Li, whose legs had both been blown off to two short stumps. He was sick in the head. I still have nightmares about him.

I tried never to look a client in the eye. I didn't pretend to like them. I closed my eyes and I often cried: this never bothered anyone. They were policemen, shopkeepers, soldiers, construction workers. Young, old. Sometimes they were truck drivers or long-distance taxi drivers who rented beds on the pavements along the central market. They were just beds, wooden platforms with mosquito nets, which people brought out at night – you could rent one for about twenty-five US cents. That was humiliating in another way.

It was common for a man to hire one of us and take us to a room where there were ten or twenty men. It was mostly Chinese men who did that. But when the same people came back again we still had to go, even if we knew what was waiting for us. If we didn't agree to go we were punished.

We wore thick white make-up, like geishas – a kind of paste we made of white face-powder from Thailand mixed into coconut oil. It made our skin paler, which was what the clients wanted, and it hid the bruises.

The worst thing was how dirty I felt all the time. Aunt Peuve's brothel was filthy, the streets were filthy, the beds were filthy. I felt I stank of sperm. I hate that smell. Sometimes, even now, I'm invaded by the stench of it, usually after I've been talking to a girl about her experiences as a prostitute. Never during – she needs me to be controlled, to listen to her. But afterwards I'm overwhelmed. I feel sick, I feel I stink – it's as if I will never be clean. I keep a cupboard full of creams but nothing takes the smell away.

I was always trying to get clean at the brothel. I'd learned in Chup to boil tamarind leaves in salt water and to wash wounds with it: I did that to myself as often as I could. The other girls didn't seem to bother. We didn't talk much either. When you're in a brothel there's only one reality, which is the clients, and nobody wants to talk about that. And Aunt Nop and Aunt Peuve didn't like us to talk among ourselves.

Grandfather came every so often to the apartment. Aunt Nop always gave him money. At first I said nothing to him – I was frightened, I think. But finally, I think the third time he came, I asked him why he had done this to me. He said it was none of my business. It was like I had no right to ask him – and I felt that, too. I had no right to a·k him, or to protest: I belonged to him, and this was just the way things were.

Occasionally Aunt Nop's husband would come to the apartment looking for money. He didn't like what she did to make it, but he didn't do anything to stop it, and he wasn't there much – he had another wife, and two children with her, and he also gambled a lot. Then he died. It was some kind of motorcycle accident, I think, about six months after I arrived in Phnom Penh. Aunt Nop had to sell her apartment to pay his debts.

One afternoon she took us back to Aunt Peuve's and left us there. Our ownership had been transferred. From now on we wouldn't just work out of Aunt Peuve's brothel, we would also sleep there, on the filthy pallets that were set up in two rows across the floor, in full view of the stairs. It was a horrible place – my skin crawls when I think of it. In the corner was where Aunt Peuve slept – she had built a small room with cinderblock walls. She kept it locked, so I never went in there. The 'room' where I was raped on that first night was where Aunt Peuve's younger sister slept, on a big bed behind a wooden partition: we often slept there, all together, during the day. There was a toilet behind a curtain, where we washed with a scoop and a basin of dirty water.

I don't remember any windows. The buildings in the alleyways behind the market were so crammed together there wasn't much daylight to be had anyway. We lit the place with oil lamps and then much later, when there was more electricity in town, I think I remember a naked lightbulb.

We cooked over a brazier in the large room with the sleeping pallets: people going up and down in the stairwell used to stop and ask what was cooking. There were people who lived up there – I think they were *motodup* drivers, people you paid to drive you through the city or do errands on a motorcycle. I never went up to have a look.

During the day the guards slept in the room with us. At night we worked. Aunt Peuve was not unpleasant to us, so long as we did as we were told. She talked to us sometimes – she was quite pretty, about thirty or forty I suppose, and she had two small children who lived with us too. She didn't have such an easy life. Li, her husband, beat her, and he used to sleep with all of us constantly.

We caught diseases, of course. But we were lucky – there was no Aids in those days. If I got sick I knew what to do because I had worked as a nurse in Chup. I bought medicine, and I washed myself with tamarind – I think that probably protected me.

I also didn't get pregnant, which really was lucky. If a girl got pregnant she had to go to Aunt Peuve's friend who did abortions. She would come back white and bleeding. But once the bleeding stopped there was no pity: it was right back to the clients, as soon as you could stand.

Sometimes clients came to Aunt Peuve's, and sometimes we stood out on the streets around the central market, which was just around the corner. Most of the clients called me '*Khmao*', insulting me just as the villagers did in Thloc Chhroy. I didn't fetch a high price; I was just a street whore. I didn't have regular customers like some of the other girls, perhaps because I didn't smile, and then of course I had dark skin.

But one time a man seemed to be interested in me. He came several times. We almost became friends. He told me that he loved me and wanted to marry me. This was about six months after we moved to Aunt Peuve's and part of me wanted to believe him – to believe that there was a way out.

I think she may have had wind of what was up: she told me she would have me beaten to death if I tried to get away before I had paid back the money she was owed. But the guards had grown used to us; they weren't as watchful. One night, when I was supposed to walk back from visiting a client, I just didn't go back. I went to meet that man.

He was about thirty I suppose, ugly-looking, but he could talk. And I wanted to trust him. The next morning he took me to the truck station. He said we should go to Poipet on the Thai border. He put me on the back of a truck that was heading for Battambang and he promised to join me there. There was another girl with me in the truck. When we got to Battambang that night the driver and the other men on the truck raped us. My client had sold us to the truck driver.

I was sick. Sick of it all. Everything revolted me. I vomited. The next day, when the truck stopped at Svay

Sisophon, I ran away. I remembered that my adoptive mother had some relatives there who came from China. I asked everyone, and finally managed to find them.

This man and his wife agreed to take me in. I minded their children, and I started to cook and do the washing for them. I thought I had found a place to stay. But after a week the wife left – she sold gold on the market, which took her away from home. When she'd been gone for a few days the cousin threatened me with acid – he used it to clean the gold. He raped me and he said he would kill me if I said anything about it to his wife.

I decided that the whole world was the same; that all men resembled each other. After about a week of this I begged him to let me go. He finally agreed. He even gave me a bit of money and a gold plate necklace. When I asked him he said I should take a truck to Battambang and stay there over night before getting a ride to Phnom Penh.

. I had already made it to Battambang when I saw his wife looking for me. She grabbed my hair in the street and accused me of having stolen her necklace. She took me to the police station, where her husband confirmed her story. They threw me in the cells: I was clearly guilty, since the necklace was in my bag.

There were three or four policemen and they said, 'If you want to get out you'll have to pay,' but I had no money – they had taken it away. They took turns beating me and raping me all night. They said this was a way to pay and they laughed about calling all their friends too. There was no point at all trying to resist. I only got hit harder, as if they expected it. In the morning they just let me go.

I had nowhere to go. I couldn't go back to Thloc Chhroy. The only person waiting for me there was Grandfather. Though I called him Father, Mam Khon had never suggested he could protect me from Grandfather. There was only Phnom Penh.

I had no money and no necklace; I convinced a collective taxi driver to give me a lift to the city. But I was only sixteen and I had 'merchandise' written on my forehead. I know now how closely taxi drivers work with the brothels: they bring in the supply of girls, as well as the clients. I suppose that taxi driver must have recognised me, or heard that I was missing – a dark girl with long hair, a Phnong savage with a scar on her face. He drove me to straight to the central market. When he stopped the car Li was waiting there, with the guards.

It was as if there was nothing at all I could do right – no way I could escape. I felt I must somehow be carrying this destiny with me, as if the sign of some devil had fallen across my life.

Li beat me with his cane and tied me naked to a bed. Anyone who came was given the pleasure of looking at me. Despite everything I'd been through I was still fundamentally modest and this experience was horrible. That night his brother and all their friends took their turn with me while I was still tied up. It went on like that for a week. I was sick, shaking with fever.

I think that was when Li discovered something I was

really afraid of. He was scientific about punishment: he wanted us completely cowed. He must have realised I wasn't terrorised by the basement room, because when I was taken down there I didn't scream helplessly like the other girls. I just glared at the guards – I thought about how one day I would kill them. And I always tried not to show pain, because I didn't want to give them the pleasure.

But one night Li dumped a bucket of live maggots on me. Hideous maggots, like the ones on meat. When he saw how much they frightened me he began putting them into my mouth, on my body, while I was sleeping. I thought they would make their way inside me, into my body. That's what I have nightmares about, even now.

After Battambang I said to myself that I had tried once to escape and I wouldn't try again. It would be the same no matter where I went. And – though I know this is a slave mentality – for all her faults, Aunt Peuve was not horrible to us so long as we cooperated.

So I told the other girls, 'It's worse outside. At least here we're protected from the police.' And from that point on I capitulated.

5

Aunt Peuve

I began doing most of the housework for Aunt Peuve. I
needed to try to keep the place clean and by doing all the
cooking and cleaning, and looking after the children, I
bought myself some peace. Aunt Peuve understood that
I had given in. She began to be much nicer to me – even
friendly. She saw that I was clean and honest. She began
leaving me alone in the house: she knew I didn't have to
be guarded any more. After a while she even began to let
me go out to run errands. She knew I'd be back.

I understand what I did then, I can recognise what
was done to me, but I don't recognise what I felt – why
I did these things. I had just given up.

There were about a dozen girls living at Aunt Peuve's
house at any time. New girls would come in and have

their spirit broken, as mine had been. Rarely, a girl would leave, to live in a special, exclusive arrangement with a client. More often a girl just didn't come back one night and we'd never learn why. Perhaps they escaped. Perhaps they were sold.

I know three girls were killed. The first time was a young girl, Srey, who went out one night with a client and one of the older girls, Chethavy. Chethavy was tall and pretty and she came from Kampong China. She had been a schoolteacher, but her husband and mother-in-law took her to the brothel.

Just before dawn one morning Chethavy came running back to the brothel. She said that she had escaped but the client had shot Srey. Aunt Peuve didn't want any of us going out – she made us shut up and called the guards to deal with it. But later that morning I went there to see. It was in an alleyway like ours, just one street away, and when I went up the stairs I saw the place – just a bare room, hardly big enough for the bed, and not even a proper door, only a curtain to shield it from the stairwell. It was like a lot of other rooms in Phnom Penh. Srey's body was gone but there was still blood on the floor.

The client was drunk and angry – we never learned any more about it. Maybe Li made him pay something to compensate for Srey's earnings.

The second girl was Sry Roat, a girl my age who arrived about six months after me. She was very pretty, with white skin, and men always picked her. I never learned who sold her to Aunt Peuve: if a girl didn't talk

I didn't ask questions. I was walled into my own silence, dead to almost any feeling, and like all the girls I knew that it was better if you never thought about that kind of thing. It was better to forget the past. You had to endure every day as it came and hope only that it wouldn't be too violent. No other kind of hope seemed even a tiny bit realistic.

But Sry Roat desperately wanted to get out. And she thought that one of the men who used to ask for her a lot really liked her. She asked him to help her escape. She didn't know he was a friend of Li.

When Li learned about Sry's plans he came upstairs and tied her up, right in front of us. We were sleeping – it must have been about ten in the morning. He tied her arms and held a pistol to the side of her head and shot her brains out of her head. The other girls were crying but I watched him. After he shot her, she fell over. Her head was hanging off the bed with the side of it half gone. He shot her again, two or three times, just for sport I think. Then he and the guards put her body in a rice sack and took it away.

The third time was much later. It must have been 1988. A policeman came in late one night. He wasn't a regular client, and it was very late, about 2 a.m. This girl – I can't even remember her name – didn't want to go with him. She was sick. He was drunk. The yelling woke us all: 'Watch, all of you, because this will happen to you too one day if you don't obey,' and bang, she was dead.

Aunt Peuve didn't say anything. Everyone was frightened of that man because he was a policeman. Everyone in the neighbourhood feared Li, too, because he had a big stock of weapons and he was known to be very violent. But even Li didn't do anything about it. The policeman left and the guards took her away in a rice sack, just like Srey. We were rubbish alive and rubbish dead. They probably threw the sack on the public dump.

Most of the time I was silent. I did what I was told. I told myself I was dead. I had no affection for anyone – not for Aunt Peuve's children, nor for any of the other girls. I had some pity. If another girl had had a really brutal time, or if she was badly hurt, sometimes I would volunteer to go to a client in her place. But mostly I felt nothing but hatred.

One time, though, I let two girls go. They were new, straight from the countryside, and they looked alike, with long, dark hair. Aunt Peuve had them tied up and they were crying. I knew what was waiting for them – the life would be taken out of them. They would die internally, like me. And for some reason I didn't want it to happen again.

They weren't the first new girls I'd seen, or even the youngest – they were about fourteen. But when Peuve went out, and left them with me, I untied them. I just said, 'Don't stay here.' I had nothing else to say – I really didn't talk then, and there wasn't anything else I needed to say. They looked at me – they didn't say anything either – and they ran.

I was punished. Li hit me hard – his children were crying, because they liked me a lot. By then Li had electrodes hooked up to a kind of car battery. They burned your skin. I still have the marks. I was taken downstairs and beaten for days, three or four I think: I felt like I was bleeding inside. Afterwards I couldn't work for a few days, and then I had to work even more to reimburse the cost – the girls cost two gold '*chi*', about eighty dollars. I never did anything like that again.

My punishment was harsh, but the way they punish prostitutes today is far worse than anything I ever had to suffer. When I was with Aunt Peuve, except for that one time with the electricity, the punishment was mainly beatings and our own fear – things like the snakes. Now I see girls in brothels with nails hammered into their skulls. That sounds unbelievable, but we have photos. Girls are chained and beaten with electric cables. They go mad. We've rescued several children from brothels who have completely lost their minds.

Recently some dead girls were found in the sewer of a brothel: they had drowned. Another time, after a fire, the police found several girls' bodies, still chained up. They know who owned that brothel – everybody does, but he isn't picked up and nothing is done about it. He has too many connections and the girls are nobodies.

The cuts and weals we see on escaped prostitutes these days are unbelievable. The clients do it, or the pimps. Maybe it's the influence of Chinese films; the pimps watch them avidly, like a lot of other men. They're full of scenes of torture.

Nowadays the girls are much younger, too. This is

because men in Cambodia will pay a thousand dollars to rape a virgin for a week – it's always a week, for a virgin. Sex with a virgin is supposed to give strength. It lengthens a man's lifespan and even lightens his skin.

To make it clear they offer true, bona fide virgins, the brothels today sell children. Often they are very young girls, five or six years old. After the week is over, they sew the girl inside – without an anaesthetic – and quickly sell her again. A virgin is supposed to scream and bleed, and this way the girl will scream and bleed again and again. They do it maybe three or four times.

Brothels that specialise in virgins for rich men are evil places. After a few months the girl drops in price and they sell her on. There's a big call for novelty, and most of the brothel-keepers have family connections – there's always a cousin in the trade, in Battambang or Poipet, who will take a girl or make a swap.

People believe sex with a virgin will stop you getting sick, which is another reason for the high price of a young girl. People use them like a medicine, to cure Aids. The little girls tear much more than grown women, and they get Aids.

At Aunt Peuve's there was no resewing and no small children. Aunt Peuve dealt in young girls, but they were never much less than twelve. When a girl came in from the countryside, she just told the clients, 'she's a new chicken,' but I don't know if that meant she got more money. I think in those days there wasn't the same market in virginity as there is now. There was a lot less money around then, under Communism.

This was just ordinary prostitution. Stinking mouths and bodies, dirty rooms, violence. The blows hurt but the act itself was much worse. Sometimes there would be only two or three men a day, sometimes many more. If there weren't enough Li would tell Aunt Peuve not to feed us so we'd try harder. If there were too many you hurt inside and out, until you managed to shut all feeling off.

It's still happening constantly, today, tonight. My story doesn't matter, except that it stands for the hundreds of other girls' stories too, and their stories are why I don't sleep at night. They haunt me.

Mom, the dark-skinned girl from Aunt Nop's house, used to go and see her mother often. She had a different kind of arrangement with Aunt Peuve. She paid Mom money and Mom used to take it over to her mother every week. Sometimes I went with her: I had nobody else to visit in Phnom Penh.

Mom's mother accused her of being lazy and she used to beat her a lot – there was never enough money to make her happy. She still rented a room from Aunt Nop, just a few streets away from where we'd all lived. Sometimes Aunt Nop would be in when we visited and she'd give me tea. I hated her and I didn't like being there, but she pretended to like me. So I sat and answered her if she asked me something.

It must have been some time in 1987 when Aunt Nop told me that Grandfather was sick. Apparently he had been coming to see her regularly, to get more money. I suppose he was extending my stay with Aunt Peuve, though in those days I had no idea what the system was – I didn't know I was collateral for an ever-swelling loan. Now, Aunt Nop said, Grandfather was ill and he was asking for me.

I didn't go back to Thloc Chhroy to see him or anything like that. I was seventeen years old by now and I had been a prostitute for almost two years. I had watched Li shoot my friend Sry Roat. I had more anger in me and I wasn't afraid of Grandfather any more. I also had no desire to return to the village. If people had been nasty to me before, when I was just a child, they would be truly evil to me now that I was a prostitute.

Aunt Nop didn't make any comment when I told her I would stay in Phnom Penh instead of visiting Grandfather. She neither approved nor disapproved: she had done her duty. Several months later, when she told me Grandfather was dead, it was the first time in years I had felt glad. I had often dreamed of killing him.

But it didn't mean I was free. Aunt Nop said I must now reimburse all of Grandfather's debts. After he died all kinds of people claimed he owed them money and I had to pay them. I don't know how to explain this, but that was just the way it was. He had looked after me, I was his 'grandchild' and I was his indentured servant, and so his debts became mine.

I didn't try to protest. I just lived from day to day and my body was nothing, of no value. I had never received money from any client – they just paid Aunt Peuve – so it made no difference to my life.

*

Mom found a man who really liked her. He was a soldier and his name was Roen. He had a wife already, but he found Mom a room to rent and gave her money. One time his wife came and slapped Mom. She threatened to have her attacked with acid, though she never did do it. Eventually, when Roen ran out of money, Mom's mother made her go back to work because Mom was pretty and could earn a lot. But before that, when she was living with her soldier, I thought Mom was lucky, with nice clothes and only one man to service.

By now I understood that I was actually paying back a fixed sum of money, and that one day that sum would be paid. I don't know if it was Mom who explained it to me, or whether it was Aunt Peuve who showed me the account. She trusted me now; she talked to me and treated me more like an equal. I was eighteen by now and more of an adult.

Aunt Peuve's business wasn't doing very well – she was down to about four girls. Li used to gamble a lot and maybe that was why things were going downhill. I had been sick with a high fever for a while. It meant I was just a cost to her – my food can't have been very expensive, but there were fewer clients and I wasn't earning much.

I had been working for her for three years when Aunt Peuve let me know I could go. It was about eight months after I heard that Grandfather had died. She didn't say it like that outright. She told me one of the clients had offered to marry me and she counselled me to accept.

This man drove a *motodup*, a motorcycle taxi, and was a really ugly piece of work, and dirty, too. There was something about him that I'd always disliked, and I always tried to avoid going with him. He was a regular client of one of the older girls, Heung. After being with him, Heung always came back bruised and hit – though that wasn't unusual, a lot of men were violent.

Perhaps it was out of kindness that Aunt Peuve suggested I marry this man, because I'm sure that by then I really had paid back Grandfather's debt many times over. But I have to doubt it was purely an expression of friendship. Maybe I was becoming less profitable to her. Actually, I wondered whether the *motodup* driver had offered to purchase me and Aunt Peuve was trying to trick me into leaving.

I turned down the offer. I didn't think I would be safer or better off with the *motodup* driver – he wasn't even rich. I knew by then that on the streets of Phnom Penh a girl is a commercial product. Even if I left Aunt Peuve, if I was poor someone would just sell me again. And that would be OK because it would make him rich.

I told Aunt Peuve I would stay. But it made me realise that there might be a way out of the brothel for me. There was nothing else I knew how to do, and nowhere else that I could go but some other place of prostitution, but I began to suspect that I could escape, like Mom had done, and I longed for it.

About a month after the *motodup* driver offered to buy me another man came along. His name was Minh. He was a businessman, involved in different kinds of trade – an ordinary client, though he wasn't as brutal as most of them.

I felt nothing at all for him: I saw only a staircase I could climb, a way out. When he asked me to come and stay at his place I started spending nights there. His shack was on the roof of a building near the river, in a neighbourhood we call 'Four Rivers', where the Tonle Sap river meets the Mekong. It was like a shed, made of random pieces of wood and metal sheeting, like a lot of other shacks all over the city. Minh fed me and looked after me for two days, and then he told me he had no money left and I would have to go out and earn some for us both. He said he was starting a business, a shop we could both work in – he was vague about it and I didn't think it was true.

We didn't have a formal arrangement. I hadn't officially left Aunt Peuve. But I began to work for Minh. He used to watch out for me on his motorcycle while I waited for a client to come by. I worked for Aunt Peuve too – for a couple of weeks I worked out of Aunt Peuve's apartment most evenings and for Minh during the day, to make money 'for us both'. Then I realised that he was lying to me just like everyone else and I stopped.

I went back to Aunt Peuve's place. Minh was really angry. Months later he was still hassling me for money. And I became even more convinced that there was only one way I could get out of prostitution. I would have to find a man who was rich.

6

Foreigners

Sometimes – very occasionally – I would go into a rage.
Maybe it was the Phnong in me: I would suddenly crack
and rebel. The first time was when I let the two girls go
and got punished so badly. The next time was right at
the end of my years with Aunt Peuve. I shot a client.

It might have been New Year's Day in 1989, because
the white people were all celebrating something. There
were a lot more white people around, suddenly, in 1988
and 1989, and they weren't Russians and East Germans,
as they'd always been. They were French and Italian and
English people who they had come to Cambodia because
the Vietnamese soldiers were leaving. There were peace
talks happening, in Paris, and the new white people were
mostly humanitarian workers from organisations like the

Red Cross. Anyway, on the night I shot the man there was a lot of shouting and laughing by drunken white people in the street – it was some kind of special day.

The client who had hired us was a man who used to always pick Mom and me. We would try to slip away from him when he came to Aunt Peuve's but it was always us he chose, though sometimes he chose other girls to come along too. He would always take us to a room where there were ten or fifteen men, and they were always drunk. One time they drugged us. They gave us something to drink and when we woke up we were covered in bruises. This man was always complaining about us to Li, too, so that we'd be beaten. He was a big man, a brute who liked to use his fists.

Mom was back at Aunt Peuve's by that time, because her soldier friend, Roen, was away, and her mother had run out of money. That night the client chose just her and me. He drove us all the way to Ken Swai, a village outside Phnom Penh – maybe it was where he was from. He was drunk and it was late, and there didn't seem to be any other men with him. He took us to a room above a bar and he kept drinking.

It was very late and he'd been drinking steadily for hours when he began to yell at us and shoot at Mom. He wasn't shooting wildly – he was sitting at the table with a gun and shooting around her to scare her, just like my husband used to do to me when I lived with him in Chup. He was angry, but he was enjoying it. Then the client went to the toilet to piss – he was so drunk he left his gun on the table. I picked it up.

71

Mom said, 'Do you know how to shoot?' I looked at her and went into the bathroom. He was frightened – he said, 'Don't do that, *Khmao*' – but I fired the gun. I was just so angry.

The bullet hit his leg. He was yelling but probably nobody could hear him because of the noise in the street. I really wanted to kill him but I thought about his wife – of course this man had a wife, and probably daughters, too. So we tied his mouth up with his scarf and left him there. He was really scared and so were we. We ran as far as we could and at dawn we found a *motodup* to take us back to the brothel.

That man did come back to Aunt Peuve's to complain eventually, but it wasn't for weeks – I think he was too frightened to do it before, or maybe he was in hospital. By that time I was already protected: I had found Dietrich.

Dietrich was a humanitarian worker with one of the big relief agencies in Phnom Penh, and one night he picked me up on the street. I saw the Toyota Landcruiser with the agency's logo on it drive slowly past me as I stood on the pavement. It circled around the block and came back and stopped.

Aunt Peuve was watching, as usual, and she handled the negotiations and took the money. It was the first time I had ever had a white client and I thought he looked strange – he was about twenty-eight, much taller than any Khmer and his hair was long in a stripe down the middle of his head and short everywhere else.

Dietrich didn't just take me to a room of some kind, either. He took me to a street stall first, because he was hungry and wanted to eat. He didn't speak more than eight words of Khmer and I certainly spoke no Swiss-German, but he bought me dinner, which no client had ever done, and tried to talk to me. He clowned around, mimicking things – he tried to make me laugh. He pushed at the corners of my mouth so I would smile. He was funny.

When he took me to the guesthouse room he'd rented it was the first time I'd ever seen a mattress. I was very unsure of myself. I didn't know what this foreigner was going to do to me; I thought maybe white people were different from Khmer. He sat down on the bed and patted it, signalling for me to sit beside him, but when I sat down it felt soft – as if something was swallowing me – and I leaped up, frightened. This client laughed again and motioned for me to go in the bathroom and wash myself.

I was glad to have a reprieve from the mattress, which was genuinely scary, but the bathroom was strange too. It was very clean but I had to look everywhere for the basin of water to wash myself from. The only water I could see amid the shiny taps and empty white containers was a tiny amount at the bottom of the toilet. I had never seen a toilet like that so I thought it must be the washing bowl. I splashed the water on my face, thinking, 'That's all the white people use to wash in?'

When I went back into the room Dietrich said to me with gestures, 'Did you shower?' and I shook my head. He came back into the bathroom and turned on a shiny thing, like a snake, and it flashed into life, spitting at me. I jumped back – that thing was evil and would hurt me for certain. I was frightened, thinking it might be a phantom of some kind and I ran out screaming. Dietrich had to explain running water to me, the pipes and the shower head. It was another world. I was scared that the water would flood everything and I would drown. Despite my fear, I tried to have a shower, all wrapped up in a towel, and leaving the door open so that I could run out if the phantom came back.

. That was the first time I ever used proper soap and I remember how good it smelled, like a flower. Soap is expensive and so the only thing we ever used was soap-flakes, the kind you wash clothes with.

After that Dietrich did pretty much what all the clients did, although he didn't hit me. Then he drove me back to Aunt Peuve's place and he gave me extra money, which no client had ever done before. It was a lot. He paid fifty US cents to Aunt Peuve for me, but he gave me twenty dollars.

Dietrich used to come looking for me at Aunt Peuve's brothel, but I could tell he didn't like doing that. Sometimes he'd send his translator for me – he was a Cambodian man who worked in the office of Dietrich's relief agency. When I was with Dietrich I would spend all night with him, in a nice room in a small hotel or at one of his friends' apartments. In the morning he would always drive me back, with money for Aunt Peuve and money for me.

Sometimes Dietrich gave me enough money so I didn't really have to work for Aunt Peuve for a few weeks. I'd give most of it to her and then go off to spend a couple of nights with other girls I knew. One of them was Heung, who was living on her own now. Aunt Peuve had thrown her out – she was at least twenty-eight, which is old for a prostitute, and sick, so she wasn't earning much money. Heung was selling herself on the street but she didn't have many clients: she could barely pay for the shack she rented from another woman, Phaly, who was also a prostitute. Their shack was on a rooftop, though it was falling apart, really barely any shelter at all.

I used to bring Heung presents and stay with her for a few nights. Or I'd visit Chetra, a girl who had left Aunt Peuve to be the live-in mistress of a Khmer shopkeeper. Chetra was from an ethnic minority like me: she was Stieng, from the hills about eighty miles south of the village where I grew up. She and I liked to eat the same food – I loved to go to her place to cook spicy chilli dishes.

After a few weeks Dietrich stopped renting hotel rooms and started taking me back to his house. He lived in a big villa near the Calmette hospital with a gate and a guard to open it. There was a porch with French columns, silk cushions on the sofa and a cleaning woman. When I first saw it I could not believe it. I was used to clients who took me to mouldy rope beds on the street.

I didn't 'love' Dietrich. He was nice, though. He was

kind, he didn't hit me, and he did his best to communicate, although he never learned much Khmer – we spoke in gestures. But I was nineteen years old and I learned a lot from him. The first time Dietrich took me to a restaurant for white people, I made a fool of myself. It was at the Hotel Blanc, a really nice hotel now. I could smell chicken – it smelled unbelievably good. I had a pretty, shiny pink dress on – I had recently had it made, but I could tell my date didn't like it.

And when I asked for chicken it came roasted – a whole thigh in one huge piece, with a knife and fork. How would I know how to eat with a knife and fork? In Cambodia we cut meat into tiny pieces and we eat with a spoon or with our fingers. I knew that if I ate Cambodian-style here, people would take me for a savage. So I bravely wielded my implements, but at each attempt to cut the chicken it wandered off to one side of the plate or the other. The more I tried, the more difficult it became. While I waited to capture it I swallowed my rice. I couldn't ask Dietrich for help because we could hardly speak to one another and he seemed to notice nothing. My frustration grew from one moment to the next. Dietrich made a sign asking me, 'Aren't you going to eat your chicken?' I shook my head. Time passed and at last the waiter took away the dish which was literally making me salivate. All night I dreamed of the poor chicken I hadn't managed to eat.

One night, when I was with Dietrich in his Landcruiser, I caught sight of my adoptive father and his younger son. They were riding on a motorcycle beside Dietrich's car and gesturing to me. Father looked wrinkled, exhausted and really poor. I asked Dietrich to stop the car and got out. Father told me he'd been looking for me – he had heard I was in a brothel. He had sold his fishing nets and his boat so he could come to Phnom Penh and search for me, he said. He wanted to take me back to the village with him, where I'd be safe.

I was flooded with shame. I was dressed indecently, in a foreigner's car – I looked like a whore and I was one. I couldn't go back to Thloc Chhroy with this good man, whom I had shamed, and face the villagers there as a Phnom Penh prostitute. I couldn't do it, and I couldn't face Father. I got back in the car as fast as I could and told Dietrich to drive off. I was so ashamed, I didn't think to give Father any money – I didn't even say a word to him. As we drove off I was crying.

When Dietrich gave me money I enjoyed the freedom it gave me and the clothes I bought. They were just trousers and T-shirts, but they were clothes that didn't say 'whore': they looked like a nice person might wear them. Still, Dietrich was a client. I couldn't count on him. He never said when we might see each other again and he was often away for weeks at a time working for his humanitarian agency. When I had to, I worked for Aunt Peuve.

But now, instead of standing by the side of the road around the central market, I went out to a hotel called the Samaki, Cambodia's most luxurious establishment. I could see there were many foreign men there and I began waiting for them at the bar. Cambodians thought my dark skin was ugly but foreigners seemed to like the colour, and also my hair, which went all the way down my back. Foreign men didn't seem to beat girls as much as Khmer clients did. They took you to nicer places. They also paid more.

But then Dietrich suggested I become his 'special friend' – he had to explain this through a translator. I would live with him and he would give me spending money. He handed me a key to his house. I didn't even go back to Aunt Peuve's place to pick up my things.

I liked the luxury and the comfort of living at Dietrich's house. It never felt like I really lived there, though. I never learned how to cook properly in his kitchen, which always frightened me, and he always ate out anyway – often with his friend Guillaume – and always European food in restaurants for foreigners, never rice and *prahoc* sauce and spices.

Still, Dietrich was a good man. He didn't like it that I cried when we had sex but we mostly did it in the dark so he didn't always notice. He was also rich – for Cambodia, anyway – and he was white, which meant he had power, and because of this nobody could bother me any more. When Minh, the man I'd lived with briefly in the rooftop shack, tracked me down and yelled at me for money, the guard at Dietrich's gate sent him away. That felt good.

But Dietrich's contract in Cambodia was drawing to a close and he had to go back to Switzerland. About six months after I first met him he brought his translator to the house again to talk to me because he wanted to be sure I would understand. He said he was leaving for ever, but that he would be glad to take me with him if I wanted to go.

It didn't seem real to me. I knew nothing about Switzerland and nothing, really, about Dietrich, though I'd lived with him for several months. My friends, Chetra and Mom, thought that perhaps he planned to sell me once we got to Europe. I too distrusted Dietrich in a way: I couldn't understand him, could never figure out why he did things. I thought that if I left Cambodia for a place where I could understand nothing at all, not even the language, I might find myself a lot worse off.

Before he left, Dietrich gave me a thousand dollars. (In Cambodia we use US dollars for large sums; the national currency, the riel, is only for small sums of money.) To me, it was an unimaginable sum of money, something like a hundred thousand dollars today. He had his translator tell me that with this money he wanted me to buy a motorcycle, go to school and maybe start up a business – he said that I should use it to make myself a new life. Dietrich didn't want me to have to go back into prostitution. He really was a decent man.

After he left I went back to Aunt Peuve's and gave her a hundred dollars. I really have no idea why I did that, but it's what I did. I suppose that, like an idiot, I thought she had feelings for me. I also gave a hundred dollars each to Mom and Chetra. I couldn't find Heung – she had left her shack and nobody knew where she'd gone. But to all the girls at Aunt Peuve's house I gave fifty dollars each. I bought them their freedom, if they wanted to take it, and that was something I never regretted.

I think that was the last time I went to Aunt Peuve's brothel. I have avoided the street ever since. When I go near it my skin crawls and I begin sweating. I don't have the strength – I always end up making a detour.

Now I had to figure out what to do next. Before leaving, Dietrich asked his friend Guillaume to look after me. Guillaume was Swiss too and I owe him as much gratitude as I owe anyone in this world. He let me stay at his villa and he found me work, cleaning for his friend Ceclilia, who was Italian. I earned twenty dollars a month. It was enough.

Guillaume took me to the Alliance Française building in town and had me sign up for French lessons there. I didn't have enough money left to pay for them, so Guillaume paid himself. But he never tried to touch me, never took any advantage: he was only being kind to another person. He is still my good friend.

I liked going to the Alliance Française. There was no uniform, of course, but I bought a dark blue skirt and a white shirt and ironed them carefully before every lesson. They meant something to me, something clean and honest, like a mask over the filth that was underneath. I had a deep desire to pretend to be a nice young student at the Alliance Française, with books under my arm.

I didn't learn much – French was hard. When Grandfather sold me to my husband in Chup I was just finishing primary school: I could read and write curly Khmer letters, but the straight letters of the Roman alphabet were very different. It was just one class a week, but little by little I began to understand words. I loved trying to learn something – I worked at it.

Sometimes I used to go out with Chetra and Mom to the nightclubs that Dietrich had taken me to, where there were a lot of foreign men. Mom was working for Aunt Peuve again and when we went dancing she would pick up clients. I met some men too. Hendrik, an American who worked in Singapore. Paolo, an Italian. It wasn't like prostitution, because these were longer relationships than just one night, but it was close.

I had been a prostitute in Phnom Penh for four years, and I didn't know how to get out of the system. I wanted to, but in my mind I was trapped in it. I wasn't worth anything.

Guillaume knew a lot of people, and he had parties. All his friends claimed to fall in love with me, which meant, of course, that they wanted to have sex. These were rich white people who worked for embassies and cultural centres or big businesses. They came to Cambodia for a year or two and they rarely spoke Khmer, just like they didn't eat local food.

But one night I met Pierre. It must have been in 1991. He was tall and nice-looking in a raggedy kind of way. He was French, about twenty-five, and he worked for a

French humanitarian agency doing lab analysis. I was twenty, and I had never met a foreigner who spoke such perfect Khmer.

Pierre asked me questions about myself. Dietrich had just tried to make me laugh, but Pierre asked me a thousand questions. He asked where I came from, how I had come to be a prostitute, why I was doing it and whether I wanted to get out. He listened. And I, who had always been silent, found that I was talking.

We talked from the early evening till 1 a.m., and I think that first night we didn't even have sex. Pierre respected me. A white man who spoke Khmer – that was really something. I may not have loved Pierre, but I thought I could live with this man. He was simple, like a Cambodian. He ate rice and *prahoc* sauce. He lived like a Cambodian – he had a room with some other foreigners in a large wooden house where the electricity often went off and the kitchen had a charcoal fire and a cold-water tap. Pierre wasn't rich, but of all the people I had ever met, he was the only one who was attentive to *me* – not to my body but to me, my life, myself.

That first night I told Pierre I wanted to get out of prostitution. I wanted to be clean and decent. I hated selling my body to strangers. But I had no skills and very little money. He asked if I wanted him to help me set up a business and the next morning he gave me a hundred dollars. He told me he wanted me to use it as a kind of start-up fund, to get a business going. He genuinely wanted to help me and I was deeply touched by that.

I was also still very shaken up from our conversation. Talking to Pierre had brought back a lot of memories and a flood of emotion. I had told him about my adoptive family – how Father had tried to look after me in Thloc Chhroy, how he'd registered me in school and how kind and good he was. When Pierre gave me the money, I suddenly thought again about how poor and tired Father had looked the day he caught sight of me in Dietrich's Landcruiser. I decided to do something good for him.

I went to the old Russian market and bought a stock of notebooks and pencils – small supplies to start a little shop. For a schoolteacher's family, it made sense to buy school supplies. But how could I get the supplies to my family? I would have to screw up my courage and go back to my village.

In my memory, Thloc Chhroy was a place where people had always looked down on me. They hated me because I was just a savage. There were a few good people, and those are the ones I want to remember, but most of the villagers had only hard blows and insults for the dark-skinned kid who fetched them heavy pails of water every morning and worked for them in the fields. I knew that these people must now know I was a prostitute, for if Father had heard it most certainly others had too. I knew they would look down on me, and perhaps even throw stones. I didn't want to go back.

But I got on a ferry that was headed for Kampong Cham. It wasn't so very far – the trip took perhaps five hours – but all the way I was tense with nerves. I made sure I would arrive in Thloc Chhroy in the evening, when most people would be eating, so I wouldn't have to see anyone.

I hadn't been back since Sophanna's wedding, when I was a fifteen-year-old nurse in Chup. Now, five years later, the village seemed somehow smaller, but richer too. Several houses had new shutters in their windows. There were even one or two big, new houses made of solid wood planks. There was a second little shop standing beside the Chinese merchant's shop, where he'd raped me. I felt a wave of hate as I walked past.

The beaten-earth paths through the village were still the same, but Father's house was pitiful. The woven palm tree walls hadn't been changed for a long time. When we were children we were always having to weave new walls or new pieces of roof out of dried coconut palm leaves, but nobody had done that for a long time. The house looked stained and worn, black where insects and rot had eaten holes in the walls. It was sinking to one side because the stilts were rotting and the rainy season hadn't come yet – the land was parched. I felt a stab of guilt and pity.

They were home, the Mother and Father I had chosen for myself, or who had chosen me. They looked old and thin and much smaller, like shrivelled versions of themselves. When I came in they were eating from a small bowl of rice soup with a bit of dried fish in it, and I saw the surprise in their faces. But they didn't say very much. Father smiled, and said 'Good to see you, Daughter.'

I gave them the big bag of school supplies that I had

bought with Pierre's money and clumsily explained what I had in mind. Mother smiled: I could see how relieved she was – it wasn't easy, living on a schoolteacher's pitiful pension. Unlike other schoolteachers in Cambodia, Mam Khon never demanded that his students pay him for the right to attend school or to pass exams. And because he was an honest man he had very little money.

Mother made a fuss over me and apologised for not having more food. She offered to go out to the merchant to buy something, but I didn't want to embarrass her – I could see she had no money.

Father had tears in his eyes, and Mother and I did too. We cried but we couldn't find any words. Memories were swirling around inside me – painful ones, and sweet ones too. I couldn't tell these good people about my life in Phnom Penh, about being pawed and beaten and raped by a long succession of dirty and contemptuous men. My life was dishonourable and ugly, and I felt I was too.

They gave me news of Soechenda: she was living in Kampong Cham, the big local town, and working for the agriculture ministry in an office there. Sothea was attending the *lycée* in Phnom Penh, but he was working for a barber to pay for his studies.

Then Sophanna came in. She was living in a shelter outside my parents' house – just a shack really, it wasn't even on stilts. She worked as a schoolteacher in a nearby village. Her husband was out but I gathered that he earned no money. All he did was feed the pigs and lie around the house. Sophanna looked thin too. She had somehow lost her looks: her pretty little mouth looked drawn and her eyes had lost their joy. She seemed far older.

Seeing how poor they had become made me want to help my family so much. Despite their poverty, Father asked me again to come and live in the village with them. He said he wanted me to be 'safe' – that was all that he said, but I understood what he meant and hung my head in shame. I knew I couldn't come back to Thloc Chhroy. There was nothing here for me. It was a hateful little village, where very few people had been kind to me before; how much worse would they be to an ex-prostitute with no money? I shook my head.

I told Father that I had met a man, a foreigner, who lived in Phnom Penh. I said he seemed good and that he had given me the money to buy the school supplies. I knew that Father wouldn't like it, but I thought perhaps he would understand. A Khmer man would beat me and abuse me because I had been in a brothel. In Cambodia I was for ever stained. A foreigner might not mind so much about my past.

Father just asked me again to stay in the village. He said, 'I don't want you to go back to the city. I'm afraid people will hurt you. Please stay here, at home.'

I thought perhaps Father would force me to stay. The next morning, before daylight, I dressed and walked to the river in my city shoes and I took the dawn ferry back to Phnom Penh.

7

The French Embassy

When I returned to Guillaume's place in Phnom Penh I found a Cambodian man there waiting for me. He was the caretaker of the building where Pierre lived and he told me that Pierre was looking for me everywhere. I learned later that Pierre had even told a friend of his that he'd found the woman he was going to marry, the most beautiful girl he had ever seen, and he wasn't going to lose her so easily. He was crazy about me.

When I went to see him, Pierre asked me if I would like to move in to his room, in the large wooden house he shared with some other foreigners from humanitarian agencies. I was nervous about this. Pierre was poor and shabby: he wasn't the rich foreigner I'd had in mind. He wasn't like Hendrik, the rich American who lived in Singapore who had once given me a hundred dollars just to spend on clothes. But Pierre spoke Khmer and that really meant something to me. He ate like a Khmer, too, and he was different from the other foreigners.

I asked Guillaume what he thought I should do. He advised me to find somebody else. He said that Pierre didn't seem to be very popular among the foreigners – probably because of his strong opinions – and that I should bide my time. It wasn't much of a recommendation. Personally, I rather liked the fact that Pierre had a big personality, but I decided to do as Guillaume suggested.

Sometimes, as we were about to make love, Pierre would stop. He said he didn't want to force me. But I couldn't get the image of sex-related violence out of my mind. There was nothing I could do to annihilate my past. Coming back to life, to some kind of innocence, felt impossible. I didn't know where my youth was, where to dig to look, if not for happiness, at least for a kind of peace. Pierre was kind, but our nights together were always difficult for me.

Then Pierre left town, to go on holiday in Vietnam with some friends. I knew that these friends didn't think much of me. They thought I was unworthy, trash he'd found on the street. Then, one day, while Pierre was gone, I saw a man I knew, a cousin of my adoptive mother. He was a big shot who worked in a government ministry and he asked me what I was doing in Phnom Penh.

I responded that I was a student – I was still attending the Alliance Française so it wasn't quite a lie. He invited me to have lunch with him, which I could hardly refuse. As we came out of the restaurant I saw a friend of Pierre's staring at me, so I stared back.

Pierre got back a few days later and when I returned to his place I found my things in a pile on the floor. He was throwing me out. He told me I would never be any good – he said that I had lied to him, that I didn't want to stop selling my body. He accused me of seeing clients while he was away.

It wasn't true. Since I'd met Pierre I hadn't slept with any other man. At that point I still hadn't yet made up my mind about staying with him but I wanted to show him that I respected him, as he showed respect for me.

When you're a whore people always think you're dishonest. They assume you're a liar and a thief. I would have left if Pierre had grown tired of me – that I would have accepted. But I hated that he would share the same opinion of me as everyone else. I wanted him to see the kind of person I was trying to become, straight and honest.

I cried. I refused to leave. I told Pierre that I had no interest in staying with him. I said I wasn't sleeping with him for money; there were plenty of richer men at Guillaume's house. And I wasn't just a prostitute. There was nothing voluntary in what I had done. I shouldn't be accused of sleeping with men when it wasn't the case. I asked him to give me the chance to prove I was not a liar.

It was while I was pleading with Pierre that I realised how much I wanted this. I wanted so badly to leave the world of prostitution far behind me. Pierre was scruffy, and sometimes strange, and he got angry a lot, but he was different from anyone else. He spoke my language and I had thought that he understood me.

I vowed to myself that if Pierre took me back I would stay with him and I would prove that I was not just a prostitute through and through.

We began living together. I didn't 'love' Pierre: sometimes I'm not even sure what the word means. But because Pierre spoke Khmer, it felt like we were a real couple – not, as with Dietrich, strangers who nodded at each other and had sex when the male required it. I stopped going to the Alliance Française. We didn't have much money and Pierre was teaching me a little French anyway.

In 1991 Pierre's contract with his humanitarian agency ended. He wanted to go back to France. I told him that if he left I wouldn't go to Europe with him, but that if he wanted to remain in Cambodia for a while I would stay with him. He said he would stay – he would go back to France just for two weeks to do some business, but he'd be back.

Pierre left me twenty dollars to last while he was away. That was OK – twenty dollars was enough for food. I spent a lot of time with the neighbours, a Cambodian family with two sweet little children. I didn't like sleeping alone in the apartment, so at night the children used to come and stay over.

But Pierre didn't come back. It had been three weeks, then four. Finally he phoned: he had been sick with malaria but he was flying back the next day. When I went to get him at the airport I had forgotten what he looked like and I greeted the wrong man. I walked up to his friend Louis – it's true they looked quite alike. In those days I still never looked Pierre straight in the eye. It took a long time for him to break me of that old habit.

Pierre told me he didn't have another contract to work in Cambodia. Instead, he announced, he was going to set up a business. His idea was to open a bar overlooking the riverfront in downtown Phnom Penh. It was where all the new foreigners seemed to want to be – Phnom Penh was suddenly full of new white people from the UN, who had come to prepare the country for elections for a new government. Pierre said soon there would be peacekeeping troops from all over the place and that you could bank on the fact that these people would be thirsty.

We moved in with a friend of Pierre's to save a little money while he looked for the right property. He found an apartment on the first two floors of a building overlooking the river. Pierre wanted to make a little café out of it, a place you could go and have breakfast, with good coffee, but where you could also drink a beer in the evening and eat food. He decorated it with palm leaves, like a village house, and there were flowers everywhere. He called it L'Inéptie – 'Nonsense'.

Pierre hired an Italian friend of his to make sandwiches and fondues, and he took on four waiters. He waited on tables too, and so did I, sometimes till 2 a.m. I told Pierre I wasn't prepared to work for free so he agreed to pay me twenty dollars a month. When I pointed out that this wasn't much he told me I was getting free room and board.

Pierre invested all his money – a few thousand dollars – to get the place into shape. And at the end of the first month he paid me. It was clean money, the first honest pay I had ever held. I went out to the market and spent it all on a sumptuous violet dress with a white lace collar and a little jacket. I thought I looked utterly beautiful in it! The Chinese man who sold it to me for twice its value played a fast one on me, but I didn't want to bargain. This little piece of happiness wasn't for haggling over. That evening, when I had stopped work, I went up to the flat and put my dress on again. I never showed that dress to anyone. It was only for me, like some magic gown that transforms everything.

One day Pierre rang his mother to tell her that he had split up with his French girlfriend and was living with me. She seemed very upset: I thought she disapproved of her son living with a Cambodian. I was disappointed. I had suffered racism all my life from the Khmers and I wanted to get away from it.

But Pierre told her, 'I don't give a damn what you think.' It shocked me to hear him talk like that. How could he say that to his own mother? In Cambodia, no matter how old you are you keep quiet in front of your parents and always show respect. This didn't seem to be true of French people.

Pierre's friend Théo owned a video camera and he suggested we make a video to introduce me to Pierre's mother. Pierre filmed me but I was paralysed with shyness. I couldn't open my mouth. I doubt his mother warmed to me.

In those days it never ceased to amaze me how much French people spoke. Cambodians are a silent people. On the other hand the French, when they hung out around the bar at L'Inéptie, talked for hours. I've never seen people talk so much. I was exhausted just listening.

In November 1991 the King returned to Cambodia. He rode through Phnom Penh in the back seat of a pink Chevrolet convertible and children waved at him in the streets. The return of the King from exile was part of the peace agreement that the United Nations had cobbled together for Cambodia. The Vietnamese agreed to withdraw from their occupation of the country, King Sihanouk returned, the UN agreed to oversee the government and hold elections and the guerrilla fighters – the Khmer Rouge and all the other military units – agreed to try to win those elections by any means possible.

Most of the Cambodians I knew were less than thrilled by these developments. We have learned to be cautious: when there is change in high places it is often not good news in low ones. When Khieu Sampan, a Khmer Rouge leader, returned to Phnom Penh in December 1991 to open an official office for the Khmer Rouge a mob attacked him and tore apart his office.

Soldiers had to rescue him in a tank. Most people feared that was just the beginning of the trouble and were worried about the clashes that the new election process would bring. Nobody believed the fighters would just turn in their guns and we would glide into a parliamentary democracy.

In 1992, twenty-two thousand foreigners arrived with UNTAC, the UN peacekeeping force. Almost everyone welcomed this huge influx of *barangs* – a Khmer term for Europeans – with their limitless money. New restaurants and bars opened almost every month in Phnom Penh to service the new foreigners' constant needs. A lot of them were prostitute bars – places that were a little nicer than the brothels where the peacekeeping troops could go to pick out girls. That business was booming, but there was no prostitution at L'Inéptie.

If a foreigner turned up with a very young girl, as often happened, Pierre would throw him out. I remember how angry he got one time when a big German man came in with a girl of twelve or thirteen – I thought there would be a fight. Perhaps that was why business wasn't very good. The place was often full, but mostly during the day, when people just hung out and talked.

I thought Pierre was brilliant. I admired him and if I ever thought of an ideal future it was to stay with him. He was a vehicle for me to escape my life and to learn new ways to live in the world, and also to be able to help my parents, but I did also respect him. I tried to love him, too, and perhaps if he had been kinder that would have worked. But Pierre was not tender – it wasn't a fairy-tale romance.

One time I caught sight of a girl I knew from the brothels. It was the Water Festival, when the flow of the Tonle Sap river reverses and the floods finally drain off the land so the rice can ripen. In Phnom Penh we celebrate with fireworks and all kinds of races, and I used to sell food and drink on the street. The girl's name was Kun Thea, and she told me she had managed to get out too – she was living with a man and they had two children. She was living just a fifteen-minute walk from L'Inéptie, and I told her to come by any time. We grew quite close.

By now I understood enough French to get by with the customers. Often the foreigners came in with Khmers who worked for them, in the various non-governmental organisations, UN agencies and peacekeeping units. It was clear to me that these Khmer had a good life. I thought it would be good if I could learn enough French to be able to do that too.

I sent money to my parents regularly. It was not money I took from Pierre – it was my own clean money, which I had earned. One time I went back to Thloc Chhroy. My old friend Chetra drove me there on the back of her motorcycle. When we arrived, in the early evening, Father was in shorts still beating the grains of rice out of a pile of rice stalks though the light was fading fast. From Sophanna's shack I could hear my sister crying out in pain and her baby son howling too. I walked in: her husband was hitting her.

I told him to stop it. He called me a whore – 'Don't try to give me any lessons, whore.' I grabbed the chopping knife from the kitchen and made a gesture like I was going to cut his head in two. He ran off.

Father probably intervened sometimes when Sophanna was beaten. I'm sure it hurt him enormously to think that he had chosen such a bad husband for her. But no, it didn't change anything very much.

I told Sophanna I thought she should get a divorce but she refused. I have no idea whether any woman in Thloc Chhroy had ever sought divorce, but to her it was unthinkable. I gave them money and returned to Phnom Penh with a heavy heart. A few months later I heard that she was pregnant with her second child.

A little later Pierre hired a new waiter, a man I didn't like. He looked down on me because I was a Phnong, even though I was the boss's partner. One time we had an argument and this waiter called me 'Khmao', so I went to Pierre. I said he had to back me up, but Pierre said, 'It's not my problem; you deal with it.' I got angry and he actually slapped me, right there in front of the waiter. That was a real setback for me: I felt I could never really trust Pierre: *barang* or no, all men were alike.

For me, it's normal to work seven days a week, but Pierre found it exhausting to keep L'Inéptie going. He needed a break. One time he took me to Kep, on the coast, near where his friend Henri worked. They met there, talked and drank all night, and next morning slept till noon, like French people do; then, with more friends, we took a boat out to Rabbit Island, just off the coast. We all slept at the house of an old woman. It was beautiful: the full moon over the water, just as it was on the banks of the Mekong in Thloc Chhroy, and the woven crab traps bobbing on the surface of the sea.

The sea itself was strange to me – I went in, with all my clothes on, like a Cambodian woman. I couldn't even bear to look at the other women, who were wearing bikinis. The water stung my skin – it was not like river-water at all, and it tasted salty. I wondered, did people put salt into the water? To make it easier for people to cook, perhaps?

Another time, Pierre said it was time for a real holiday. He left L'Inéptie to a friend of his and told me we were going to Siem Reap to visit the thousand-year-old temples of Angkor. I knew nothing about them; I only knew that the silhouette of the Angkor Wat temple was printed on our riel notes.

We took a boat out of Phnom Penh and moved upriver, to cross the great lake where the fishing people live out on the water in movable, floating villages. The trip took all night. In Siem Reap we stayed in a house rented by a friend of Pierre's who worked for an NGO. The Cambodians who owned the house were very nice to me. They didn't see me as trash picked up in the street, they saw me as the companion of a white man, somebody who deserved respect.

I was dumbstruck by Angkor Wat. The ruins were beautiful, but more moving to me was the way they were

embraced and surrounded by thick forest. I had completely forgotten the forest, the huge trees and leaves of
my childhood in the hills of Mondulkiri. Here were vast
palaces and walkways with even bigger trees growing
straight out of them, broad and gnarled with vines, and
almost as high as you could see, their roots forming a
towering frame around the carved stone walls. I felt a
sudden sense of recognition so strong I could barely keep
still. We couldn't go everywhere we wanted to because
of the landmines, but I could tell that the forest was
deep and strong all around us.

We spent about fifteen days visiting the temples. Pierre
seemed to know all about them, and lectured me on
which king had built every one. I was amazed that I, a
Cambodian, was so ignorant and he, this foreigner, so
knowledgeable. I asked him if he'd lived in Cambodia in
a previous life. Pierre said that he had read books on
Cambodian history and that if I could learn enough
French I could read them too. He looked at me quizzi-
cally when he said it – I would struggle to read *that* sort
of French.

In Cambodia, there's nothing unusual about three
people riding on one motorcycle, and Pierre hired a man
to drive us around. Sometimes we had to get off and
push the motorcycle through the rutted paths in the
thick forest. We went as far as Banteay Srei, a small-scale
temple in red stone about twelve miles into the forest. As
we drove back down the paths I plunged into reminis-
cences and buried sensations. I asked Pierre to stop for a
while. He quickly grew restless. But I would have stayed

there for ever, remembering what a forest sounds like, the noisy bird-calls and the cool, deep smells.

Pierre decided that we should make the journey back by to Phnom Penh by plane. I had never gone up in a plane before and I didn't trust the idea: I have never been able to understand how an aeroplane actually works. I spent the night thinking about it, eaten up by worry. By the time we got to the airport I was a complete mess and when I saw the plane close up it looked to me like a metal bird, a tin can, some kind of joke. Pierre had to push me down into my seat and fasten my seatbelt, and when he did I felt even more imprisoned. It felt like being tied down in the brothel. During take-off and landing I was in a state and when we finally arrived in Phnom Penh I was green with panic and nausea. I could barely stand up.

When we got back my friend Kun Thea came to see me. I couldn't believe the change in her: she had always claimed her family life was happy. Now she told me that her husband had a mistress, that he beat her and that he had called her a whore in front of their children. She said she didn't care about living any longer and asked me to look after her children if anything happened to her. I tried to talk her out of it, but three days later I heard that she had killed herself with pills.

I wondered if it is ever really possible to clear the past completely, or whether you will always be haunted by what has been done to you and what you have done.

In February 1993, after L'Inéptie had been going for

about fifteen months, Pierre told me it wasn't making enough money. Neither he nor I had ever run a business and I guess we weren't very good at it. Pierre thought trouble was coming. The elections were being organised for May and Pierre said nobody knew what would happen, whether the government would ever give up power, and what kind of violence, even war, might flare up. Pierre said it was time for us to go to France.

I didn't feel ready for this huge new change, but at the same time I did want to see all the things had Pierre talked about – he said the world was much bigger than I had ever thought. I could already speak a little basic French so I thought it wouldn't be too hard, and I thought that if I went to France for a while I could come back and work as a translator or something. A lot of Cambodians were nervous about the political situation in those days and would have leaped at the chance to get out. I could get a passport and a visa – but only if Pierre and I were married.

That's how we decided to take the plunge: just for convenience. I didn't want to get married at all. I don't even like the sound of the Khmer wedding music – nothing about marriage attracted me. To me it was like a chain, a prison. In Cambodia, once you're married your husband owns you.

After Pierre sold L'Inéptie he went to the French Consulate to get all the forms we would have to fill in in order to get married, and for my visa. They all asked for my birth date which, of course, I didn't know. I told Pierre it was some time in 1970 and he wrote '1 April' because, he said, it was a kind of joke. It made me angry – I crossed it out and wrote '2 April'. I did the same thing with the date for our wedding: Pierre wrote down 8 May, which is a French holiday and also the date of Pierre's first, brief marriage to a French woman, so it annoyed me some more. I struck it out and put '10 May'.

For my name I wrote 'Somaly Mam'. It was the truest name of all – Lost in the Forest – and anyway, Somaly was what Pierre called me. It had been years since anyone called me Aya, or just plain *Khmao*. I called myself by the name my adoptive father gave me: his name, which I was proud to carry.

We went to the French embassy to be married. This was before they built the new embassy – in those days it was an old colonial building with a red roof and jack-fruit trees. It was impressive to be going there, but to me getting married was really part of the visa process. I didn't dress any special way or invite anyone. I answered questions and I said what Pierre told me to say and then we signed the papers. Pierre dealt with most of it.

Afterwards Pierre's friend Renaud wanted us to have a little celebration. We ate in an Indian restaurant with some friends, then went to a nightclub that played mostly African music, for the Cameroonian peacekeeping troops. I remember how amazed people were when the first contingent of peacekeepers arrived from Cameroon, their skin so dark they looked like spirits.

We left Cambodia a few days later. I took Pierre to Thloc Chhroy to see my parents and to talk to them. It was no longer a problem for me to appear in the village in the broad light of day. Everything was different now that I was coming back to the village with money and a white man. Everyone seemed to remember what close friends we had been as children, and how sweet a child they'd always thought I was.

Father wasn't glad that I was leaving Cambodia, as I knew he wouldn't be, and I don't suppose he was overjoyed to meet Pierre. He nodded and said very little. I told him I would be back. Mother asked Pierre not to beat me, to love me and look after me; she asked him what my life would be like far away in France. Pierre told them, 'Don't worry, your daughter can look after herself.' My parents both wept when we left.

Six days later we left for France. I had no idea what I might be getting into. A few days earlier Pierre and I had had a fight, and when we left I was still seething with anger. As I packed my suitcase I slipped a sharp knife inside it. 'If Pierre tries to sell me when we get to France,' I said to myself, 'I'll kill him.' You never know.

8

France

In the aeroplane I struggled to stay calm. I'm proud and I didn't want to show Pierre how frightened I was. We arrived in Malaysia, where we discovered that our connecting flight to Paris was delayed. The airline said they would put us up in a hotel.

To leave the Kuala Lumpur airport you had to use an escalator. I refused point-blank. There was no way I was going to step on this rolling metal serpent. Pierre was exasperated – he had to drag me on to it. In the streets I saw buildings higher than the tallest trees in the forest. Pierre said they were 'skyscrapers', and I thought he must mean it literally. Everything astonished me; it was all so modern.

Our hotel room was on the twenty-eighth floor. To get

there we had to take the lift – when the doors closed it felt like being in a coffin. From our hotel room the people looked tiny, like insects – it was terrifying. Pierre went into the bathroom and ran a bath full of bubbles. He told me I would like it, that I should go inside, but I wouldn't do it. I was afraid of the bubbles and I had never taken a bath before, or even washed in hot water. Then there was another plane. I was more relaxed by now. It was longer: we stopped in Dubai. At the Dubai airport I saw how Muslims live – not the Cham like Grandfather, but the real ones, with the women covered all in black, shut away inside their own clothes in such a hot country. I felt sorry for them.

When we arrived in France we went straight to the house of Pierre's Aunt Jeanine, in the suburbs. When we walked outside in the crisp May air I thought they had somehow put air-conditioning on outdoors. To please me, Aunt Jeanine had decided to cook rice. In Cambodia we cook rice for an hour or more: on coals, it simmers slowly. When I saw her plunging little plastic packages into boiling water I thought she was mad and even more so when, after few minutes, she took it out and put butter on it. It looked awful, half-boiled, half-raw: it was swollen, much fatter than our rice, which is nutty and fragrant. From respect for the rice seedlings I ate it all. I loved the ham, though, and the bread – the bread was marvellous.

Then Pierre took off for a couple of days. He said he had to see some friends and disappeared. Jeanine was out most of the day and I didn't know what to do – I was too unsure of my few words of French to go out, and I was frightened of getting lost. I thought perhaps my friends were right – Pierre did have plans to sell me. I told myself I had to be strong: I had to show Pierre what I was made of. ·:

Finally, on his return, Pierre suggested that we visit Paris. We were in a distant suburb and had to take the train and then the Métro. All these things were new to me, incomprehensible and disturbing. In Cambodia trains move at the speed of a walking man. This train raced along two thin rails, looking as if it might slip off at any moment; and the Métro was underground, it hurtled through the dark earth superfast.

I had heard that Paris was the most beautiful city in the world, but I didn't think so. There was hardly any green and the city seemed choked and dead, with buildings tightly packed together. There was no space anywhere. Even the Eiffel Tower didn't thrill me. It looked like a pile of old iron, nothing like as splendid or as moving as Angkor Wat. The most surprising thing was to see how people behaved with their dogs. There were dogs inside restaurants and apartments. Cambodian dogs live outside – to us, they're dirty animals.

I also watched people getting money out of a sort of big box in the wall. 'So that's how they do it,' I said to myself. 'When they need it, people just go and fetch money from the box – what a good idea.' I folded a piece of paper and slipped it into the slot. Nothing happened. Pierre laughed and explained about bank cards and the whole system, which seems extraordinary to me even today.

We went to shops too, and saw masses of pointy shoes. That was an eye-opener. My Cambodian clothes looked dismal in comparison.

We were invited to dinner at the house of Pierre's Uncle Jean. Pierre had warned me that his family was rather conservative. Jean came to fetch me in a nice car – Pierre was somewhere else – and put his seatbelt on. He gestured but I shook my head to show I didn't understand. I pulled the seatbelt when he showed me, but he had to latch it for me. When we arrived at his house, Jean got out and closed his door. I was still in the car and had no idea how to unfasten the belt. He gestured but I didn't know what to do – he had to unfasten me himself.

I felt I had not just failed a test; I didn't even know what the test was. At dinner the food was a mystery. Some of it was simply revolting. Fish in cream sauce – I had to force myself to swallow. I thought the cheeses smelled horrible, too. The French seemed to eat vast quantities of everything, but especially meat. I could hardly believe how much they put inside themselves every day.

I was overcome by it all: the succession of dishes, the abundance and the fact that people left food on their plates. They cut off the fat and left it; they left meat around the bones and didn't suck them; then they cheerfully threw it all away, along with the thick fish skin. We could have fed whole families in Cambodia just with these leftovers. In Thloc Chhroy we only ate meat once or twice a year, on special holidays. My mother would buy two hundred grams of pork for twenty people and chop it up very finely, as a kind of flavouring. We were grateful for every grain of rice.

That evening went on for a long time. At one or two in the morning everyone was still talking. Pierre didn't translate anything for me. I was lost, jet-lagged and hungry. Everyone smiled at me but there was no contact at all. I felt like Pierre's little savage, sitting at the end of the table without uttering a word.

We went to Nice to visit Pierre's mother. She had a yappy little dog, Tatou, who barked the whole time and ate from a plate at the table. To me it was truly disgusting. The plan was for us to live with Pierre's mother for a while, until Pierre found a job, but I felt out of place. I was worried that everyone thought I was a gold-digging foreigner who had seduced Pierre, so I tried to stay out of the way. Pierre was out most of the time and I just sat in our room with no one to talk to and nothing to do.

I needed to take French lessons but we didn't have much money. I had brought a French–Khmer dictionary with me from Cambodia and I asked Pierre to recommend a children's book for me to read. Pierre told me again that I'd never manage it, but he bought me a copy of Joseph Kessel's *Le Lion*. He was right – it was far too difficult for me. I told myself I had to do it and every night I wrote down words I had to learn.

Pierre went off to Paris to look for work while I

stayed behind in Nice with his mother. One day I found a copy of the local paper, *Nice-Matin*. Looking through it, I came upon the classified section. I saw the word *'emploi'* and looked it up in the dictionary – it meant 'jobs'. I pieced together a few ads with the aid of my dictionary and I saw that people were looking for cleaners and maids. I realised that even with little French I might be able to find work.

I asked my mother-in-law how to do it and she took me to a temp agency and dropped me off. I was left to walk in by myself. There were all kinds of foreigners inside there. I explained to the director that I wanted to work. I told him, *'Je veux travailler,'* in a loud voice and he got the message. He smiled broadly and told me I could start the next morning. I would be a cleaner at the Hotel Hibiscus on the Promenade des Anglais.

That night, when Pierre phoned from Paris, I told him I had found work. He couldn't believe it – that I would find a job before him, without even speaking proper French. I was just happy when I heard about the salary. With 2500 francs a month, I thought, I could begin sending money home to my parents.

The next morning my mother-in-law drove me to the hotel and I carefully memorised the route into the centre of town. A Madame Josiane met me and gave me a dozen rooms to clean. She didn't show me how, and I had no idea how to make a bed properly. I also didn't know how to use the vacuum cleaner. It was like a long snake and roared at me – I was always frightened that it would suck up my feet or climb up my body. I had to make a great inner effort to control it. I was also puzzled by the variety of cleaning products.

That first day I didn't even try to use the vacuum cleaner and I made the bed all wrong. When Madame Josiane came back she said, '*Ooh la la*,' and laughed, then showed me how to do it, using sign language. By the end of the day I could tell she was pleased with my work. I cleaned behind and under the furniture without being told and I didn't stop for lunch, as the other cleaners did – I didn't even stop work to drink. And I never minded working weekends.

At the end of the month I got my first pay cheque. I had only been in France for two months and I'd already earned 2500 francs, such a huge sum of money. In Cambodia that would be a fortune, perhaps a year's pay. But what was I to do with this piece of paper, a cheque? Pierre explained that he would open a joint bank account for us and that I should deposit it there. That made me nervous. What if we divorced? Pierre could take all my money. I told him that I wanted to open an account in my own name and he told me, 'You're a real Chinese woman.'

I don't have a habit of trusting men, and I never really trusted Pierre. He would go out and not come back until five in the morning. You never know.

Sometimes the hotel clients tipped me. I remember one elderly woman: after I had helped her put her clothes away she took my face in her hands and said, '*Mignonne*'. I didn't know the word, and I asked her to write it down so that I could look it up in my dictionary. She thought I was pretty! I looked at myself in the mirror and thought she must be making fun of me.

After a couple of months of working at the Hotel Hibiscus I realised that I could make more money at another hotel. The Hibiscus paid badly and I had to work seven days a week. Also, some of the male hotel clients bothered me. I suppose they saw me as a little Asian girl who wouldn't make a fuss. I didn't want to put up with that kind of thing any more, and now I knew I didn't have to.

I went to a hotel called the Blue Vacation. Their clientele was mainly retired people, who stayed for several weeks at a time. This gave me the chance to get to know them a little, and those elderly people were the ones who really taught me French. Some of them were very kind: they called me their 'little Chinese princess'. I saw that French people lump all Asians together, but I didn't mind it – Cambodians do the same with foreigners. To us they're all *barang*.

I like old people. They deserve to be looked after with respect. Sometimes, if their bones ached, I would rub their legs and massage their ankles. They appreciated that. They began joking with the hotel management that the pretty, pleasant girl was cleaning bedrooms while all the disagreeable staff waited tables in the restaurant. So I was told to clean rooms only in the morning; at lunch I would wait tables.

I got lots of tips, but that made all the other staff jealous. They called me 'Chink'. My orders were never cooked on time. Finally, after a few weeks, I cracked. I grabbed a knife in the kitchen and shouted at one girl, 'If you keep going I'll stick this in your belly.' I was surprised that I knew how to say it. It didn't make me any friends but it bought me peace – after that they left me alone.

My mother-in-law was still hostile. I cleaned for her and sometimes I offered to cook, but she didn't like my food and she never spoke to me much. It was always clear that she would prefer to be alone with her son – she constantly tried to drive a wedge between us. When I got home after work I didn't dare make myself lunch, even though I was always hungry.

I lost a lot of weight. One time she fed Pierre and me eggs and spinach, and gave meat to her dog. I put up with everything, because in Cambodian custom you have to put up with everything your mother-in-law does and not complain to your husband. A Khmer husband will always take his mother's side against his wife, so it's best to endure in silence.

But after we had lived in Pierre's mother's apartment for four months some friends of hers came to visit. They had children with them – the kind that jump on everything and destroy stuff. I said to one of the little ones, 'Don't jump about like that. When the old lady comes back she won't be happy.' To me this wasn't any kind of insult. In Cambodia we say 'Yeh' for any elderly woman – it's a term of respect. But when my mother-in-law got home the mother of the little monsters told her I'd called her 'the old woman', and my mother-in-law was furious. She slapped me and locked me in my room.

I didn't understand what I had done, and was horribly upset. I explained everything to Pierre when he got back. To my surprise he understood immediately and said it was time for us to find another place to live.

Pierre had just found a temporary job as a lab technician, which made it easier. We rented a studio on the ground floor of an apartment building, with a little garden outside. The first night I had a nightmare. The garden was squirming with slugs, like the maggots Aunt Peuve's guards used to throw on my face and body. I screamed uncontrollably, and spent the rest of the night wearing socks, several pairs of pyjama bottoms, gloves and a hat. I didn't want any of those slugs to touch me.

But those nightmares were growing rare. The central market in Phnom Penh was far away and I was starting to get used to a new life. One afternoon I left work early and decided to visit Nice, which I barely knew. I took the bus. I got off at a bus stop at random and walked around in an area I didn't know. I got lost and phoned Pierre, but he told me to work it out myself, like a big girl – if I'd got there I could always get back. It was harsh, but I knew that Pierre was just trying to teach me to look after myself.

Since the place where we lived was close to the sea I told myself that if I walked along the coast I'd manage to find my way home. I walked until my feet ached and when I looked up I found I was standing near a sign written in Khmer. *Ku tieu Phnom Penh* – noodle soup,

Phnom Penh-style. I thought I was dreaming. I went in and started speaking to the people in Khmer. They responded. I was overwhelmed: tears came to my eyes. I sat down and drank two bowls of good, spicy soup. Then I had a coffee with condensed milk poured on to ice cubes, the way we drink it in Cambodia.

In this way I made contact with the Khmer community in Nice. The owners of the restaurant said they had a Khmer group and that they were planning a small festival with Cambodian *apsara* dances to celebrate the New Year in April. I had learned those dances as a child in Thloc Chhroy, so they asked me to join the performance.

Then Pierre's contract as a lab technician ended – it was only temporary and it wasn't renewed. I was earning about 3000 francs a month at the hotel but our one-room apartment alone cost us 2500. Pierre had met someone who wanted to start up a laboratory in Cambodia, but the negotiations were dragging on. I needed to find work and I now knew that there were a lot of Asian restaurants along the coast.

I knocked on all kinds of doors. A Chinese man from Cambodia agreed to give me a job washing up in his restaurant. He even said that I could eat rice there before starting work. I wouldn't be working officially – he didn't want to pay employee charges to the state – but I was just glad of the money.

Sometimes I got paid, sometimes I didn't. I used to leave the apartment at six a.m., walk ten kilometres to the hotel and work there till three p.m., coming home at four; then at six I would leave again to go to the restaurant.

Pierre would collect me at one or two in the morning. He always complained that I smelled of the kitchen, and finally I told him I'd walk home alone.

Pierre was never a comforting man – he's no good at tenderness. He's straightforward and his angles are sharp and sometimes cut. There are advantages to this: Pierre taught me to fend for myself and he made me speak – he hated it when I was mute.

One summer day at the hotel I fainted. The doctor said it was overworked and that I should take a two-week break. But I don't know how to do nothing – two days later I was back. The truth is, I enjoyed working at the Blue Vacation. I liked looking after elderly people and they seemed to care for me.

After the summer rush was over the hotel informed me that it was my turn to take a holiday. I had worked for a year and, according to my pay slips, I had accrued four weeks of leave. I had never gone on holiday before – I had no idea you had a right to such a thing and I couldn't imagine doing what the French people did in Nice. They mostly walked around in colourful clothes and spent money, it seemed to me. We didn't have any, so that was out.

A cousin of my mother-in-law suggested we could get temporary work doing the *vendange* – the wine harvest. He told us he knew a man who could give us work in Villefranche, harvesting Beaujolais grapes for a month. Pierre thought it would give us some fresh air and a change of ideas, so we went.

Monsieur Marcel was nice enough about it, but when he saw me he said, 'She'll never make it.' I was just a little thing – I weighed about forty kilos and he was at least double that. But I told Pierre, 'He'll see.' I was used to physical work.

Pierre couldn't bear the cold, the humidity, the earth that stuck to his feet. He just couldn't do the work, but I loved it. It was beautiful to be outdoors and smell the earth, feel grapes in my hand, and I thought cutting grapes was a lot easier than harvesting rice. Pierre was proud of me, and so was Monsieur Marcel. He used to call me 'our little Chink', but he meant it in the nicest possible way.

At set hours we all stopped to take a break and eat. That's where I learned to eat cheese and cold sausage. In other words, to become altogether French. I discovered really good country cooking, soups and tasty dishes very far from the plastic sachets of rice. Monsieur Marcel and his family were really good people. After the harvest was done there I wanted to continue, so we went to Gevrey-Chambertin in Burgundy. The manager there was so pleased with me that he gave me a bottle of wine to take home.

But we were leaving France. We had decided to return to Cambodia. Pierre had worked out another job there, with a humanitarian agency. This time he would be working for Médecins Sans Frontières. Pierre had concluded that he wasn't made to live in France – it just didn't agree with him. He wanted adventure, something less settled than a small medical analysis lab in Nice.

I was proud to be going home. I knew that I had changed a lot during the eighteen months we'd lived in France. I had worked in honest jobs. I had learned to look people in the eye and communicate with them directly, as an equal. I knew that when I went back to Cambodia people would no longer look down on me as a white man's whore. They would see me as a white man's *wife*. I was like the people we call '*Khmer de France*' – Cambodians who live in France and come back on holiday, with money and power, and with the white person's sense of self-assurance. I might have a dark skin and I might still look like a savage, but I had proved that I wasn't stupid and I no longer felt I was worthless.

9

Kratié

Pierre's new job was in Kratié, an old colonial town on a bend of the Mekong river, about two hundred miles north-east of Phnom Penh. In November 1994 we moved into a room in a big house near the river that was rented by several people who worked for Médecins Sans Frontières. Almost all of the white MSF team members lived together – it was cheaper that way, and they paid a Cambodian woman to clean and cook.

Pierre didn't want to pay the extra for the cook – he said it was too expensive and, anyway, he didn't want to spend all his time talking to other French people. This was what Pierre was like: if we were in Cambodia he wanted to live like a local. I liked that attitude of his. He would rather eat rice at roadside stalls with the

Cambodian staff of MSF than share roast chicken with the doctors.

Still, there was a good atmosphere at the MSF house. I used to help the cook clean up – she was an older woman, about fifty, and her name was Veasna, but everyone called her Yvonne because that was easier. At first she was surprised that I helped her. She thought that because I was a *Khmer de France* I would think I was superior. I told her I wasn't really a *Khmer de France*, but I didn't tell her anything about my past.

I went to see my adoptive parents soon after we arrived. We met in Kampong Cham, which was not too far away; my sister Soechenda was living there, and I wanted to see her and her new baby. Soechenda had married a man of her own choice: after she got her school leaving certificate she went to a training college in Kampong Cham and she married another of the students there. I had heard that both of them worked in the agriculture ministry now.

I was shocked by their living conditions. The house Soechenda and her husband lived in with their three children was pitiful. They were really poor. Soechenda had recently stopped working because their salaries hadn't been paid for so long, and they had recently been burgled.

The next person to arrive was Sophanna, and I was shocked again when I saw her – she was so thin and somehow old, not pretty and young at all any more. She had brought her five-year-old son with her and her daughter Ning, a beautiful little girl aged three and a half.

Then my parents arrived, both of them on the back of an ancient motorcycle-taxi, thin and somehow shrivelled. They all looked so sad, and when they saw each other everyone began crying. I felt a rush of love and pity for them – they had never complained. When they had written to me in France they had always said everything at home was fine and never once asked me for money as most families would.

I thought to myself, 'I know why I'm back; it is to look after these people.' This family had held out its hand to me and taken me in, these people were everything I had, and I would never abandon them again.

Soechenda had nothing in the house to eat, not even rice – just a couple of sweet potatoes – and her boys were thin. I went out and bought a fifty-kilo bag of rice and all kinds of food: chicken, and fish to make fish soup. I bought a lot, but they ate it all; they were so hungry they could hardly restrain themselves.

I stayed two nights. The first night Father asked me if I wanted to go to a hotel and I said no – what an insult. I may have been to France but I was still the same person – I told him my name was still Somaly, the name he'd given me when I was a child in Thloc Chhroy. But in fact I was shocked at how dirty everything was; I was no longer used to washing under a sarong using the outside shower and the bed was unbelievably uncomfortable. I had changed.

When I got back to Kratié I told Pierre I wanted to help my family and he said, 'It's your money, do what you want.' I gave them money to buy supplies, to set up a business. My parents had lived for a long time off the hundred dollars of school supplies that I had given them. Long before it became a slogan, Father always used to tell us in Thloc Chhroy, 'It is better to give a fishing net than a fish.'

During the day I often went to the government clinic where Médecins Sans Frontières had set up its headquarters. I used to help out with translation because most of the MSF team didn't speak any Khmer. One day a traditional healer was brought in. He was protesting – he didn't want to go to the government hospital – but two younger-looking people had brought him in, too weak to resist. The doctors called me because he really needed treatment but he didn't want to take it.

When I asked if I could help the old man began talking to me in his own language. I realised that he recognised me in some way, and I also realised that I could more or less understand the gist of what he was saying. Maybe his language resembled the one spoken in my forest, I don't know. But I started thinking about my childhood again for the first time in a long time – remembering what it was like. I had forgotten Phnong. That night I couldn't sleep. I realised I had no idea where I came from or who I was.

I had to decide what to do now that we were back in Cambodia. Money didn't matter to me – we had enough. I asked Pierre's boss at the Médecins Sans Frontières clinic if I could work as a volunteer there every morning. After all, I had been trained as a midwife in Chup – as trained as anyone was in those days, in Cambodian hospitals. And I could speak French and Khmer: that was in itself useful.

I began working in the clinic as an assistant to the team that treated sexually transmitted diseases. I worked with a fat nurse I didn't like much. Behind the doctors' backs she was always telling the patients, in Khmer, that they had to pay her for the treatments, even though it wasn't true. I applied treatments, washed wounds and helped clients understand how to look after themselves. They had gonorrhoea, canker-sores, genital warts.

Most of the people who came to the clinic were men. Some of them looked shamefaced but most just seemed angry. I hated them really. I knew they got these diseases buying and raping prostitutes. But I wanted them healed because I knew they were also infecting those prostitutes, and their wives, so I looked after them.

One day a girl came in. She was about eighteen years old and I saw immediately that she was a prostitute. I also knew that she would lie about it. What 'broken woman' could go to a respectable hospital in Cambodia and be treated properly?

I saw how my colleague dealt with her, hostile and scornful, and I took her aside and spoke to her very gently. I explained the treatment and I talked to her about sexually transmitted disease – I said she should try to keep clean and use condoms, and I told her about HIV infection. Aids had been around in Europe for over a decade, but in 1994 the epidemic had only recently begun in Cambodia. (Today, we have among the highest rates of Aids infection in Asia.)

I told that first girl that she should tell the others, if they needed treatment, that they should come to the clinic any morning. I would be there and I would see that they were looked after. After that, girls from the brothels began coming to the clinic in small groups. They were sixteen, seventeen years old. They weren't children, but they were young. Some of them looked at me with sweetness and a kind of hope, but for most of them it was resignation and a great deal of pain.

I knew these girls: they were me. I knew exactly what their lives were like. I found it was no longer possible for me to sleep at night, back in the Médecins Sans Frontières house by the river. I thought every night about those girls leaving the hospital, sick, to go back to the places where that same evening they would be beaten and raped.

I felt I didn't have a choice: I needed to help them get out of the life they were imprisoned in, streets away from me. This was something I could do that few other people could, and I had to do it.

I knew where the girls would be because I knew my way around their world and I knew how to communicate with them. The words themselves weren't as important as the feeling between us. When a victim meets another victim there's a look of understanding that is very meaningful. I was connected to these girls and they trusted me.

Most of them told me they had no soap to wash with

and I knew that was true: I had never had soap. They told me that if their clients did use condoms they were cheap Thai ones in all kinds of strange shapes that used to tear all the time. So I started there. I talked to Pierre's boss at MSF and asked him to give me a stock of condoms that I could distribute to prostitutes, and I asked for dozens of bars of soap. I argued that they might not be medical supplies, but they were important for preventing illness too.

He sighed – it was difficult for MSF to do this kind of thing because it's an organisation that focuses on emergency humanitarian relief, not preventive work on sexually transmitted disease. Still, I don't know how he did it but he got me a supply of condoms and an information pack about preventing HIV. He said he drew the line at buying me bars of soap – I would just have to manage on my own.

I went out to the market and bought some. Then, rather than distributing the condoms and soap only at the hospital, to girls who were already sick, I began to go to the brothels and give them out there, to everybody. I thought this made more sense.

The brothels in Kratié were just like the brothels in Phnom Penh. They weren't in clapped-out buildings near the marketplace: these were little shanties on stilts in the mud by the river, on the outskirts of town. But in every other respect they were just as dirty, and just as brutal, as the brothels I'd known. Walking towards them I would start to sweat, but I had to do it, even though being there made me want to vomit.

I used to pretend to be a nurse from Médecins Sans Frontières. I dressed like a *Khmer de France* and came in with an official air and a box of condoms. I told the *meebons* that I wanted to help keep the girls healthy, and that it was in their own interest that the girls be free of disease. They could only agree. Also, I think they were a little afraid of me: a *Khmer de France*, the wife of a white foreigner. They didn't dare stop me.

The first morning, I found one girl who was so small I thought she must be aged about twelve, though she said she was sixteen. A client had torn off her nipple and the wound was infected. I told the *meebon* that she should let me take the girl to the hospital to be treated. That turned out to be easy: it was in the *meebon*'s interest to keep her slaves in good condition and this way she didn't have to spend a cent.

I sat with the girl in the clinic and made sure the nurses treated her properly. She was cheerful and grateful, and my heart tore that evening, when I had to take her back.

That happened a few more times, and I realised that I could do this more often. You can't look at a girl who's badly hurt and not want to get her help. If I managed to get the girls back to the brothels by evening so they could work, the *meebons* would let me bring them to hospital in a taxi. I'm not Mother Teresa, but I needed to do this. Knowing the way those girls were living, I had to try to help them.

I asked Médecins Sans Frontières to let me have a car and a driver so I could bring some of the sickest girls to the clinic every morning. In frustration, when it looked as though MSF wouldn't make any decision to help me, I took the wife of Pierre's boss to the brothels so she could see for herself. Her name was Marie-Louise and she was a doctor too, and a really good woman. She saw the battered girls in scummy places, their wounds and scars, and she was horrified. She couldn't believe how people treated other human beings. By the time we came back to the MSF office, she was speechless. Marie-Louise made sure that I received the use of a car.

France had changed me. I was not afraid of people any more. I began spending most of the day in the brothel neighbourhoods of Kratié. It wasn't just about distributing condoms and information about HIV, or about ferrying girls to hospital. It was about being with these girls, connecting with them in a deeper way.

When I was in Aunt Peuve's brothel there were many times when I needed someone to help me – even just someone who would put her arms around me when I cried. For me there had been no one, though I was lucky in other ways. Now I needed to be that person for others.

The girls in Kratié were mostly debt slaves, as I once was. They were paying back a loan taken out by their parents or relatives. Some of them had agreed to do it. This is Cambodia: if you are a girl you owe obedience to your parents. If your family requires you to sell your body on the side of the road so that your younger brother can go to school – or so your mother can gamble – that is what you do.

A few of the girls had been sold outright. Those were the ones who lived in the nastiest places, where the owners were more hostile and the brothels more heavily guarded, and many of the girls were very young. They were captives, and I couldn't take them out to the hospital. But other brothels were not as heavily guarded.

The pimps know their livestock won't try to escape. A girl's will is easily broken and she quickly learns she has nowhere to run. They couldn't go back to their homes because they were no longer welcome there. They had no skills, no way to support themselves on their own. They were condemned to sell themselves more or less for ever. I felt the panic of it, the echo of my own experience.

The first girl I helped to escape was dark-skinned like me. She had straight hair all the way down her back. She was sixteen and she had been a prostitute for over a year. She was guarded, but I had to help her.

I found a tailor in Sanbo, a village about ten miles up the river from Kratié. It wasn't far, but I hoped it would be far enough. This woman was willing to take girls in and train them as seamstresses for a hundred dollars each. I asked Pierre for the money. He gave it to me – to his great credit, Pierre almost never complained about this kind of thing, no matter how much I spent.

I went back to the brothel and told the *meebon* that this girl had to come to the clinic the next day, for more treatment. But when we were alone I told the girl not to come. I didn't trust the fat nurse, my colleague – she liked money too much. I said she should meet me at my house and I would take her to the village. When the *meebon* and her guards came to the clinic to look for her nobody had seen her and my fat colleague told the guards she must have just escaped – this happens sometimes. They went away.

Sanbo was far enough away to escape their notice. I paid for two more girls, then another two – I sent them to learn sewing from this seamstress and I gave them a small living allowance. I wasn't buying them out of prostitution, because I didn't have that kind of money. But I was giving them a way out if they could manage to leave.

I had been doing this for a couple of months when one of the pimps in the neighbourhood put a gun to my head. I knew him. He was an old man called Mr Eng. I hadn't encouraged any of his girls to leave. The prostitutes in this old man's brothel were heavily guarded and he never let them out.

I was going to Mr Eng's brothel to give out condoms and talk, but before I'd begun climbing up the ladder to his stilt-house, he stepped out of the chair where he'd been dozing in a singlet with a gun in his hand. He held it against my head and told me to get out or he would shoot me.

I just looked at him. I don't know where I got the courage. I said, 'If you kill me then your wife, your children, all of you will go to prison, because I am protected. You know who I am. All of you will be killed.'

And he put the gun down. I was a *Khmer de France* and a white man's wife.

When I told Pierre about it later he said I should go to the police station to file a proper complaint, like a foreigner would do. I discovered that the provincial police chief was the brother of Yvonne, the woman who cooked and cleaned at the MSF team's house. Mr Eng was arrested and I had no more trouble for a while.

I knew that what was needed was a place for prostitutes to live and be looked after once they managed to escape. Pierre's salary wasn't limitless and I knew just how many more girls there were. I also thought that, with money, there might be some way to rescue the girls who were captives. They would need somewhere safe to live – somewhere the pimps wouldn't get them. They needed training. I started to write down notes, in Khmer, about what I thought this should look like – I was thinking of some kind of charity.

Then I began feeling ill. It never occurred to me that I might be pregnant. All those years as a prostitute it had never happened, and I just assumed I couldn't ever be. To be sure, I was also taking the pill. When I realised that was why I had been feeling so terrible I felt panic.

I thought I didn't want children. They are so vulnerable. They feel so much pain and it is impossible to protect them. I felt I would never know how to look after a child properly because I had never had a mother. But Pierre was delighted. He told me, 'Nature will look after you.' It was a little unrealistic, but sweet.

Pierre began helping me with my idea for a charity to help prostitutes. He and his Dutch friend Piet, who worked with MSF, started writing the statutes. Then Pierre landed a new job in Phnom Penh, with an American relief agency. He would be earning a lot more money and he told me he'd decided to accept.

10

New Beginnings

I was pregnant when we moved to Phnom Penh, and I found us a two-bedroom house on the outskirts of the city, in a neighbourhood called Tuol Kok. Houses were cheaper there, and they had gardens, but it wasn't one of the places the white foreigners had begun living – it was a Cambodian neighbourhood. I had no idea it was also becoming a concentration of brothels.

But I realised soon enough. Right near our house was a brothel they called the 'Broken Coconut' – *coconut*, in Khmer, is another word for a woman's secret place. The *meebon* stood outside it, shouting at the girls if they didn't look lively enough. They were so young. I couldn't see a girl older than about nineteen, and many as young as twelve.

All along the main road heading towards the city, for almost a mile, were filthy shacks where girls with painted faces beckoned at men on the roadside. These girls were mostly for local use: they were for *motodup* drivers, construction-workers, labourers. But there were also a number of brothels on that road that were a little more specialised. They specialised in younger children. Cambodians called it Antenna Street, after the tall radio-transmitter tower, but foreigners had begun calling it '*la rue des petites fleurs*' – the road of little flowers – because there were so many young girls on sale.

A few days after we moved in to Tuol Kok, a young policeman came by to register us as new residents. This was still the system in those days and since Pierre was foreign I suppose we merited a special home visit. The policeman was a young boy, about nineteen, and he looked hungry. I served him tea and some fish soup, and he told me a little about himself. His name was Srieng.

I was about six months pregnant but I couldn't just sit at home doing nothing. I'm not that kind of person. And it was impossible to ignore the misery of the brothels. I began distributing condoms, just as I had in Kratié, and taking girls to the clinic – I pretended to be a health worker from Médecins Sans Frontières, which was not a great idea, I know, but I didn't have a better one.

I had to steel myself to go back into the dank, filthy alleyways behind the central market where I used to work. I never did manage to go back to the place where Aunt Peuve's brothel had been. It was too alive with memories – it made me feel ill to go nearby.

I don't know if people recognised me on the street. Probably not. I was dressed differently and I had a completely different air about me. Who would connect a self-assured, well-dressed pregnant woman to the dismal, scrawny ghost called '*Black*', or Aya? I didn't go looking for anyone I knew – I was pretty sure everyone had gone.

Phnom Penh had changed enormously in just two and a half years. It was far richer, far more crowded. There were building sites everywhere. The brothels had changed too. Aunt Peuve's brothel and the other establishments had been hidden in alleyways behind the street. Now they were right out front. They were official.

The worst places, without question, were in Svey Pak. We had a car – a rattling pale blue Camry that Pierre had bought for eight hundred dollars – and I used to drive there. Six miles out of the city, it was a whole neighbourhood of brothels, again clustered around the main road. In Svey Pak there were shacks, too, but there were also other brothels in concrete houses, with high gates and walls. They looked like fortresses and it was obvious they were armed: every business in Phnom Penh had a weapon. Most of these places wouldn't let me in. Many of the girls inside were captives, and some of them were very young children. Svey Pak specialised in ethnic-Vietnamese girls, pale and beautiful, and in virgins.

Some of the children were very young – ten years old, sometimes younger still. I had never seen that before and it shook me. They were often badly hurt. I began

132

going out to the brothels every day, bringing girls to the MSF clinic or to the hospital where Pierre worked.

Sophanna's daughter, Ning, was very sick. She was about six years old, and since they'd moved to Phnom Penh she'd been ill. Pierre and I took her to the hospital and it turned out she had tuberculosis. She was hospitalised. She came out of hospital but she was still convalescing when, one day, Sophanna came to see me, white as a sheet.

She told me her husband was planning to give Ning to a neighbour, a woman who had offered to take Ning in since she had no children. She had even offered him money. He said that since Ning was always sick this was a good solution. Sophanna came and begged me to find a way out, and so, when I was eight months pregnant, Pierre and I decided to have Ning come and live with us. She was the sweetest child in the world, a truly endearing little girl, and we already adored her anyway.

The time was coming for me to give birth, but I was still ill at ease with the idea of having a child. There was a creature growing inside me, which moved and kicked, and soon it would need me, but I felt paralysed by the thought of being a mother to someone. I had never had a mother, and I painfully felt that lack. To be a mother myself felt impossible. Pierre didn't help: he said I looked grotesque, and called me 'Truck' because I was so big.

I'd been having nightmares for months with horrific images of the women I'd 'helped' through labour when I was a nurse in Chup. I told Pierre I didn't want to have anything to do with any Cambodian hospital. Cambodia had become a place where everything was for sale, even the doctors' diplomas. He told me no problem, I could give birth in the Thai capital, Bangkok.

I flew to Bangkok for a routine visit, two weeks before the birth date. Pierre's mother met me there. She was much nicer to me now, and we grew quite close. It was a very clean, very crisp, very technical hospital, but the whole procedure didn't make me feel any better about having a child. I couldn't understand the doctor – he spoke only Thai and English, and in those days I didn't speak English.

The doctor told me the contractions had already begun. It was all over very quickly – I gave birth before Pierre even arrived. Afterwards they handed me the baby. The room was dark. I held this warm, beautiful little creature whose name we had already decided on – Adana – and she looked into my eyes.

Something happened to me that night. It was almost like my life began again, a new life. This was my baby, my child, which had come out of my body like I came out of my mother's body, the mother I can't remember and never will. I looked at her all night long crying, 'My little baby, I don't want you to have a life like mine.' I told her, 'I will never leave you,' and that I would keep her safe.

We went back to Phnom Penh. My mother-in-law was enchanted by baby Adana. It seemed now that everything was forgiven, because I had produced a grandchild. And Pierre, too, was delighted. When we went for a walk with our little girls, Ning and Adana, he told me I was beautiful and I was happy.

When Adana was about a month old an American man, Robert Deutsch, contacted me. He said it was urgent. Robert had a group called PADEK, which worked with squatters – poor people who were being evicted – and he told me there was a woman with him who said her daughter had been sold into a brothel. She wanted her daughter back and Robert thought perhaps I could help her in some way.

The girl was about thirteen and her name was Srey. Her mother told me she suspected her sister-in-law's friend had sold her. I went back to where they lived and it seemed this woman was suspect: she didn't work but she sometimes had large sums of money, the neighbours said. Her brother was a policeman, they added.

When I got home I went over to the police station near my house and found Srieng, the young policeman I'd met. I explained what we were up to and I asked him to keep an eye on this woman, to follow her around for a little while and keep his mouth shut about it. He agreed unreservedly – he was a very decent man, and the idea of a child in a brothel against her will sickened him.

Srieng came back and told me he'd watched the woman go to a brothel in Tuol Kok, right near my house. I told him to go back there the next day and pretend to be a client. He would ask if there were any new girls and try to find out if one was called Srey. He did, and the *meebon* told him, 'She's too sick to see clients right now.'

I talked about it with Robert, and he said we should both go to the police. Srey's mother was just a poor woman and the police were never going to do anything about her complaint if she acted alone. But if Robert and I made formal complaints on behalf of our legal organisations the police might feel obliged to take action – that was our only hope to get Srey out.

We made so much fuss about it that the police agreed to raid the brothel. I think they didn't want to lose face. In those days few policemen supported our work. Too many of them were involved in the sex trade themselves: they worked as guards or went to the brothels as clients. Many of them were even investors.

That first raid was a farce. There were half a dozen policemen with me and Robert, and the girl's mother. As we went in the front door the pimps and most of the girls were fleeing out the back. But Srey, the girl we had come for, was still inside. She was as white as a sheet and sweating on a filthy little bed on the floor. She was feverish, almost incoherent. In the space of a few weeks, the pimps had addicted her to some kind of drug. I think it was methamphetamine.

We took Srey to the police station to tell her story and file charges. She could hardly stand. She left with her mother. I visited her the next day and got her some medicine. But she was going through withdrawal, pissing on the floor, and it was clear her mother couldn't deal with her and was trying to hide her from the neighbours. A few days later she asked me to take Srey – she didn't want her own daughter any more.

Srey was the first victim who came to live with us. We had nowhere to take the girls and no money to set up a centre, but we had two bedrooms and a living room. It wasn't large, but there was space enough.

In early 1996 Pierre, Eric and I finalised our project to create a charity to fund a proper centre to help prostitutes. We had decided to call it something mild – we knew we had to avoid attracting too much attention to the girls who would be living there. We settled on AFESIP – *'Agir pour les Femmes en Situation Précaire'* (Acting for Women in Distressing Situations). This could mean anyone; it carried no stigma of prostitution.

We took our project to the European Union office in Phnom Penh. We were looking for funds. Three months later we had no response, and when we called the secretary said our papers couldn't be traced. When we went back to submit the paperwork again the EU representative was there. She asked us, 'What is it that you actually want?'

We explained the project to her and she said, 'But there are no prostitutes in Cambodia.' She had been in the country for at least a year.

I'm not a diplomat. 'Madam,' I said, 'you're living in a world of air-conditioned hotels and offices. This isn't an air-conditioned country. Go outdoors and take a look around.'

We didn't get any money from the EU. We didn't get

any from anyone. All the big international organisations that were in Cambodia to fund grass-roots projects like ours knew about our project, but helping prostitutes didn't seem to be a priority. Sometimes, if a journalist wanted to write about the traffic in sex slaves in Cambodia, these organisations would send the reporters to me. But AFESIP was never quoted in the article – the big organisation would take all the credit.

Pierre's salary had once seemed princely, but his monthly three-thousand-dollar pay cheque was now completely absorbed by our needs and my work. I began working for an estate agent, trying to make a little extra money by finding houses for the foreigners who were now flooding into Cambodia. What we needed was a lot more money – enough to start up a proper centre where former prostitutes could live and learn to stand on their feet again – but at least this way I could make a little extra, enough to fund the girls in our house.

My job was to find houses for foreigners, and I looked for places with charm, with gardens – not the featureless concrete villas that developers were slapping up all over town. I understood what foreigners wanted, because in some ways I was now partly foreign myself.

One afternoon I knocked on the door of a small house that lay behind a beautiful Cambodian garden, with orchids hanging in a banyan tree. An old man lived there. Renting his house out was the last thing he wanted, but we got talking anyway. He asked me in for tea.

He was an intellectual and he'd been through every

kind of revolution and change in his life, and suffering too: it was marked on his face. He said, 'In Cambodia we're like frogs in front of the king. When the king orders it, we poke our heads above water and sing. When he signals we go back into the water. But if we poke our heads out without having been invited to the king cuts them off with his sword.

'I've seen everything and lived everything,' he told me. 'It's all useless. When you're young, as you are, you're enthusiastic. You want to understand a great many things. It's no use. I fought all my life and for nothing; now I wait for death. The only thing to hope for in this world is the peace you need to look after your own garden.'

I understand him, and I think about his words often. When you're a frog it's best to keep your head low: you don't try to change the world. I only want to change this small life that I see standing in front of me, which is suffering. I want to change this small real thing that is the destiny of one little girl. And then another, and another, because if I didn't I wouldn't be able to live with myself.

In August 1996 a big conference on the sexual exploitation of children took place in Stockholm, and several journalists wrote about the situation in Cambodia. After that the big international aid agencies seemed more interested in our plans for AFESIP, and one UN agency promised us funds.

They were a long time coming. By now Pierre and I had several girls living with us. One was pregnant, two had been addicted to drugs by the pimps and another had two children under the age of five. They all slept in our spare bedroom, Pierre and I slept with Adana and Ning in our room and if there was too much crying Pierre would try to get some sleep on a camp bed in the corridor.

It was a lot to take and Pierre was becoming exasperated by this continuing invasion of our home. After a series of sleepless nights he exploded one day, and told me that if we couldn't find a better solution the girls would have to leave. In desperation I went to Robert again. He talked to John Anderson at Save the Children UK, and they decided to lend us a house, which would be our first centre.

It was a small wooden house in north-west Phnom Penh, on a tiny plot of land. I could hardly believe our luck. At last we would have somewhere to house and feed the traumatised women and girls who so badly needed a refuge. Robert gave us six thousand dollars from PADEK funds.

We needed somebody to help run this place, to cook and to live there, to keep it organised. We didn't have the money to pay a salary, and who would work for free? I thought of my adoptive mother. She looked after people. I knew that she, too, had once been in a brothel, even though we had never spoken of it. I knew she would never look down on the girls in our care.

I went to Thloc Chhroy to talk to her about it. By the time I finished she had tears in her eyes and, wordlessly, began putting her clothes into a case. Father was quite surprised by this: he had no plans to move to Phnom Penh. But he agreed that Mother should come back with me and work for a while at the new AFESIP shelter.

I had other news too. One of my real estate clients had asked me to find a man to act as a caretaker and guard his house from burglary – a live-in guard is a normal expense for many people in Phnom Penh. I suggested Sophanna's husband could take the job. It was eighty dollars a month, and I knew Sophanna could do with the money.

Our shelter began as just that – a shelter, a place of refuge. It was a one-room house on stilts, and everyone slept together on mats on the bare floor. Dietrich's friend Guillaume had given me ten sewing machines, but there was no room for them. We had to set them up on the bare earth underneath the house.

The sewing machines were crucial. Mother could teach the girls to cook, but I knew they also needed a more marketable skill. A trained tailor, who knew how to draw a pattern and fit a dress, could make money – honest money – and hold her head high.

But I couldn't afford to pay for a sewing teacher. In Phnom Penh, tailors were asking four hundred dollars a month to train one apprentice. Finally, after thinking about it for a long time, I asked Sophanna if she would teach sewing. She was always a good tailor, and used to teaching. She knew I couldn't pay her, but she wanted to move to Phnom Penh anyway – she had learned that her husband was fooling around with other women.

I truly disliked my brother-in-law. He was a brute to Sophanna and never did a stroke of work. Pierre was always mocking him: he called him 'Huh', because he could barely string five words together.

We also hired a woman to do the accounts. She was the only one of us who was paid, and her salary was tiny, I think fifty dollars a month. We had enough money to pay for a few months' worth of electricity, food and medical treatment; for a long time, healthcare was our biggest expense.

We held an official opening ceremony on 8 March 1997 – International Women's Day. By then we were sheltering about a dozen women. I was very nervous. I had invited my heroine to the ceremony, but I wasn't sure she would come. Men Sam On was the head of a government body called the Central Administration Commission, as well as a number of women's associations, and she was a fighter. During the Khmer Rouge years she had been indoctrinated and enrolled in the militia like all the other young people but she'd fled into the forest and become a guerrilla, fighting the Khmer Rouge, and the Vietnamese-backed government had made her a Cabinet minister. Sometimes, when I was in Chup, I would see photographs of her in a newspaper – a small woman, pretty, smiling, wearing military fatigues.

Men Sam On came to the ceremony with a whole entourage of staff and bodyguards. She was very simple and seemed genuinely interested in our work; she signed our guestbook. When it was time for me to make my speech I could hardly talk for emotion – I really messed up my speech. But I was so proud. That was a great, great day for me. My two dreams were to open a women's shelter and to meet Men Sam On, and now both had come true.

11

Guardian Angels

I was still doing social work in the brothels, distributing condoms and health information and taking girls to clinics. This was useful work in itself, but it was also a kind of cover because I could encourage girls to escape the clutches of their pimps and come to our shelter in secret.

I was also working with the police from time to time. I began informing them whenever I heard about a girl who had been sold or kidnapped and was being held under guard. We would pressure the police to stage a raid on the brothel, and then Pierre or I, representing AFESIP, would go along on the raid as observers. That way the police would release the girl into the custody of AFESIP instead of taking her to a cell.

But the whole procedure was often extremely difficult. The police in Cambodia are not like the police in Europe. Especially in those days, many police officers worked hand in glove with the pimps. Sometimes they took money from them in return for 'protection', and sometimes they beat up clients who refused to pay. Some policemen even owned brothels, and many more were regular clients.

Every so often we would come across a decent policeman – someone like Srieng, who had compassion for the girls who were being abducted and abused. Often these men were new to the force, with no power to change anything, but if a family came to the station to report a stolen daughter they would alert me. Then I would dress up in my *Khmer de France* clothes and come to the station to file a formal complaint in the name of AFESIP, just like a white person would. That sometimes got the process moving, because it was more difficult to ignore.

By the end of 1996 we had twenty women living in the shelter. We had gone on perhaps a dozen police raids to save girls who were chained and guarded in horrible conditions. It was becoming difficult for me to go into the brothels as a social worker because people had begun to recognise me. I was shoved around and threatened.

Meanwhile, a woman I had known in Kratié had also moved to Phnom Penh. Chan Meng worked as a translator. She was a woman of great intelligence and compassion who had suffered a great deal. Though we rarely talked about it, I knew that she had lost her husband and children under the Khmer Rouge. I asked her to join me as a social worker and investigator, working in the brothels together. She's still with AFESIP today.

In 1997 a French journalist, Claude Sampère, heard about my work. He was in Cambodia filming a story about landmines for his program, *Envoyé Spécial*. I had a pretty low opinion of journalists in those days – I had spent days taking reporters through brothels in Phnom Penh, translating long and painful conversations for them, only to find AFESIP was never quoted and only the most titillating details were used.

But Claude Sampère was different. He and his team got up at 6 a.m. to accompany us on our rounds. When he interviewed the girls in our little shelter I saw him crying. I'd never seen anything like that. In those days I was still very suspicious of men – I thought they were all basically rapists.

One of the girls Sampère filmed was Sokha. She was from a refugee family – her parents had tried to leave Cambodia but she'd grown up in a refugee camp in Thailand that was run by the Khmer Rouge, and when they came back to Cambodia they had nothing. They were beggars in Phnom Penh when Sokha's stepfather raped her and then sold her to a brothel. She was nine years old at the time; by the time we rescued her from the brothel she was twelve. It was very hard for her to talk to a man about what happened to her, but Claude was very careful, very respectful.

Guardian Angels

Another girl Claude Sampère interviewed was Tom
Dy. She was a girl I found in the road one afternoon,
south of the Royal Palace. She was dirty, with her hair
clumped with mud, and frighteningly thin, and people
were throwing stones at her. Her head was bleeding, she
had sarcomas on her skin from Aids and she looked
half-dead. I thought she was about thirty or thirty-five. I
asked the driver to stop, and I put my arms around her
and took her into the car.

The driver said, 'Are you mad? She's filthy, she has
lice, Aids – don't touch her,' and he looked truly dis-
gusted. But I took her to our shelter and washed her
myself – I didn't want anyone else to look after her. I
tried to bring her to the hospital but the nurses and
everyone else glared at her. She told me she was just seventeen.

I brought her back to the shelter and talked to Pierre.
He used his contacts to get her tuberculosis medication
and other expensive drugs. Every morning I washed
Tom Dy and dressed her wounds with antiseptic. She
told me she had been a prostitute since the age of nine.
The pimps put her out on the street and threw stones at
her when she became too sick to work. With our care,
she put on weight and became like the chief of the
whole centre. Tom Dy was such a positive person: she
used to help a lot around the centre, cooking and cleaning, and chivvying everyone along, looking after the
younger girls if they didn't want to eat or became
depressed.

Tom Dy told Claude that her dream was to work

with AFESIP, to help the other girls. But she knew she wouldn't make it. She knew she had Aids. I knew it too, of course, and I knew that it meant she was going to die, though I didn't care to think about it. Claude seemed deeply affected by their conversation.

He and his crew also accompanied us on a police raid. We were looking for the daughter of Mrs Ly, a Vietnamese woman. Because she was Vietnamese the police wouldn't help her: the Khmers hate the Vietnamese even more than they hate the Chinese, and, anyway, she had no money. Mrs Ly told us that her daughter Loan had left the village where they lived to become a waitress, but now she feared that she had been sold into prostitution. She had heard she was working in Svay Pak.

Because the police wouldn't help her Mrs Ly went to Svay Pak herself. She walked around the street waving a small black and white photo of her fourteen-year-old daughter. One young man pointed to one of the brothels. She knocked, but the *meebon* sent her away.

After Mrs Ly came to us we went to the police to ask for permission for Claude Sampère's crew to film in Svay Pak. It was a Saturday, which was probably a mistake, because the police don't like to work on Saturdays. Also, it gave them plenty of time to warn the brothel owners. When we finally managed to get a permit for a raid on Monday evening there was nobody at the brothel. No girls, no pimps. Svay Pak was clean.

Pierre and I were furious with the police and we threatened to hold a press conference to expose their double-dealing. They rallied and arrested one of the brothel owners. Somehow they forced him to confess where Loan had been taken. But when we got there the house was closed up – these people, too, had been forewarned. How were we to work with the police in such conditions?

Despite the locked door we refused to leave. Finally we saw some girls trying to run away, coming out of another house down the street – many of the brothels in Svay Pak are connected by tunnels. Among the girls was Loan. When she saw her mother they both wept. We filed charges at the police station.

Before they left, Claude's team gave Loan and her mother a little money and they went back to Vietnam. It was done discreetly, without any passports; Mrs Ly knew a place where they could sneak across the border. We were still new to these matters in those days; there seemed no better way to do it.

I began to receive threats. Men would phone our house in the middle of the night and threaten me or my family if I didn't stay at home. I received letters that said, 'Leave Phnom Penh or you will die.' One day, when I was in the neighbourhood around the central market, a man drove alongside me on a big black motorcycle, the kind we call dog-bikes. He held a pistol against my side and said, 'Leave. I won't kill you but somebody else will.'

I suppose he was a contract killer who had been hired to eliminate me, but for some reason he didn't want to do it. Perhaps I had helped his sister or some other girl he knew. So he warned me instead.

I took that warning seriously. It felt different from the threatening calls and letters. The cold metal feel of the gun against my skin was very real. That evening I locked everything, windows and doors. I began pacing around the house every night, waiting for the sounds that meant a gunman was outside. I was most afraid for my family – for Ning and Adana. I didn't know what those people might do to my two little girls. I was becoming a little unhinged.

Pierre said it was time to take a break. He took me and the children to Laos, where he had friends who could lend me a house. He said it was just for a while, until things blew over. In those days Cambodians couldn't travel easily because they needed visas which were almost impossible to get, but because I was married to a Frenchman I was French and I could get a visa easily. I left the AFESIP shelter in the hands of my mother, and she and my adoptive father came to the airport to wave me goodbye.

The night before I left I wrote a letter to the Cambodian Prime Minister, Hun Sen. It was like throwing a needle into a pile of dried rice stalks – I thought it was hopeless. But I was angry and I needed to tell someone in authority that this should not be happening. I said the traffickers had threatened to roast my baby like a chicken, and that I should not be driven out of my country in fear of my life because I wanted to improve the lives of women who were being kept and traded as slaves.

*

The night we arrived in Laos I had a dream. I saw my adoptive parents' house in Thloc Chhroy burning. I woke Pierre and told him, 'We have to go home.' He was irritated. He told me to stop behaving like a superstitious old Khmer witch – 'Try to live in reality,' he snapped at me. Still, he promised that when he got back to Cambodia he would find out whether anything had happened.

My adoptive mother was at the airport when Pierre arrived and he could see that she was very upset. He said, 'What's going on – has the house burned down or something?' and she started to cry. She said, 'How do you know?'

The evening I left Phnom Penh someone went to Thloc Chhroy and put petrol all round the house where my adoptive parents lived. They burned it down, with everything inside it. I suppose they assumed that if I wasn't in Phnom Penh I had gone there. Perhaps someone watched my car drive away from my house, with the children and the luggage, and figured out that was must be where we had gone.

It took just ten minutes for my parents' house and everything in it to burn down to nothing. It was only made of dried leaves and bamboo. Because they had gone to the airport to see me off my adoptive parents weren't inside. However, there was an elderly man there, looking after the house while my father was gone, because of course it didn't have a proper lock. The neighbours pulled him out of the blaze. He was hospitalised, but he never fully recovered.

I now knew that the threats against me were real. But I couldn't stop my work. I was in danger, but so were thousands of girls in brothels. I was safe, in Laos, but they were not.

Then I received a response to my letter to the Prime Minister. A little black girl from a tiny village had written to the Prime Minister of the Kingdom, and this man actually wrote back. Hun Sen wrote that the police were investigating the arson of my parents' house, and he asked me to continue my work.

I felt proud to receive such an acknowledgement. And I feel I should say here that although many Cambodian officials are shockingly corrupt, and some of them are simply evil, I have also at times received support for my work from certain people in the Cambodian government. Without them none of what we do would be possible.

I decided to return to Phnom Penh. The holiday in Laos had done me good. It calmed me down. I vowed to be more careful in the future and I hired a driver who was a former policeman to be my bodyguard.

When Claude Sampère's programme aired in 1998 he invited me to France to talk about my work. Pierre and the children came along – little Ning, who was seven and a half, and Adana. Before we left Tom Dy asked me not to go. She hung on to me and cried. She begged me, 'Don't go. If you're not here, I'll die and I don't want to die without you.'

She didn't seem very sick – in fact she had just begun

to really put on weight. I told her she wasn't dying and that we wouldn't be gone for long. I promised to buy her a present. She asked for something pretty to wear in her hair.

Then, the day before we left, Tom Dy was hospitalised. She had some kind of galloping infection and a high fever. When I took her to the hospital she asked me if I loved her and cried in my arms. She kissed me and begged me not to go.

I thought about her every day during our trip to Paris. Phone calls were expensive and so I had no news of her for two weeks. One afternoon Claude offered to take me out to find something for Tom Dy. He truly is an exceptional man, as well as a fine reporter. We were in a department store when my phone rang: Tom Dy was dead. She had died alone, in the hospital.

I raged and wept. This sweet seventeen-year-old girl, who had been sold by her parents into prostitution, who had been beaten and raped for several years, had now died from her ill-treatment at the hands of people who had no compassion, no human feeling for anyone but themselves.

There is nothing that can excuse the sex slave industry in Cambodia. I am no big thinker, but I think even Pol Pot cannot be seen as an excuse.

After Claude's programme was shown congratulatory phone calls came from everywhere. But the funding situation at AFESIP was becoming critical. Claude took me to see Emma Bonino, who was then the European

Commissioner for Humanitarian Affairs, running the European Union's massively wealthy aid agency, ECHO. Emma Bonino was a world-class politician, and she happened to be in Paris that week.

When we arrived at her Paris office, Emma Bonino was shouting into the phone – a blonde Italian woman, tiny but with ferocious energy. I shrank back, but Claude said to me, 'Don't worry. She's like that – she shouts. But her heart is in the right place.'

Emma Bonino already knew about our work. She spoke to me briefly, and made a couple more phone calls in Italian, chain-smoking furiously throughout. Then after barking orders at some underling she turned to me again and put her arm round my shoulder. She said, 'You'll be all right.'

I was astonished by the energy that emanated from this small, smiling woman, who could shout down the line and at the same time show me such kindness. She is a rock.

Of course that one visit wasn't the end of our struggle. We had to go to Brussels to talk to the bureaucrats in the European Commission. It was my first visit to Brussels and Pierre came with me; we looked like scruffy refugees, dragging our luggage around in the rain. I didn't have a pullover and I was cold; I was wearing two pairs of socks in my cheap shoes and my feet were bleeding.

The bureaucrats looked down on us with barely disguised disdain: me with my twisted shoes; Pierre with his lopsided grin; our worn suitcases in the corner, since we had just got off the train. Apparently we didn't have proper appointments. We were shunted from office to office. Finally we did manage to get some subsidies out of ECHO but the funding stopped after a year or two – we never found out why.

12

The Prince of Asturias and the Village of Thloc Chhroy

When funds began coming in to AFESIP from the European Union and from UNICEF, the first thing we did was start building a new shelter about ten miles outside Phnom Penh. AFESIP's wooden house in Phnom Penh was much too small: by this time we had more than thirty women and girls sleeping in one room. They were young, almost all of them under twenty-two, and some of them were children. They had very different levels of schooling – many of them couldn't read or write. They were also traumatised. They had nightmares and suffered from drug withdrawal. They were suicidal, depressed, mute or uncontrollably angry.

We began building the new centre in 1998. We planned to call it after Tom Dy. We wanted to put up a series of buildings on a piece of land AFESIP had bought, near a village about ten miles south-west of the city. I wanted to have a large covered room for the sewing classes and a separate room where a full-time schoolteacher could hold small classes in literacy and basic maths. We planned several spacious bedrooms with room for ten women to lay down their mats, and separate cupboards for every person.

Then, in June 1998, while we were building the Tom Dy Centre, I was awarded the Prince of Asturias Prize. Pierre took the phone call: he told me that the heir to the throne of Spain had chosen me to receive a special award for promoting humanitarian values. Neither of us had ever heard of this prize and we had no idea how they had heard of us; but we quickly learned that it was an enormously prestigious award and carried with it the almost unimaginable sum of five million pesetas, about forty thousand dollars.

To collect the prize we went to Spain with five-year-old Adana. Ning was at school and my adoptive mother looked after her while we were away. We travelled first class, which I had never done before. I found it meant that we were treated like kings, even though we looked just as scruffy and as ordinary as ever. When we got to Oviedo, the capital of the Spanish principality of Asturias, we were told that I would be making a speech that night. I hadn't prepared anything and I've always been terrified by intellectuals or any well-dressed crowd.

157

We were welcomed into a grand reception hall, where TV crews and photographers were waiting. The Prince of Spain introduced us. The beautiful African woman standing near me was Graça Machel, the wife of Nelson Mandela and a great and good woman in her own right. Behind me was Rigoberta Menchú, who had already won the Nobel Peace Prize for her work in Guatemala: even I had heard of her. Emma Bonino was there too – she waved at me and sent me an encouraging smile. There were eight women who were receiving awards for their work to promote the rights of women and children. I felt smaller and smaller.

I was so nervous I could barely understand what the Prince was saying, but what I heard was very moving. He talked about the indifference of Western countries to the horrible cruelty of life in other parts of the world, where there is such pitiless abuse of women and children. When it was my turn I closed my eyes and just began talking about the situation of women in Cambodia.

I talked about my own life and about the girls imprisoned in brothels as slaves. I talked about how badly they are treated, the violence that they must endure. I said people talk about the gentle smile of Cambodian girls, but that smile isn't real.

I had no idea I could talk in front of a crowd for that long. When I finished there was thunderous applause. The lights came on slowly and I saw that some of the people in the audience were crying. I felt spent, but I also felt that I had achieved something important. After that television reporters wanted to interview me – there was a huge crush – but Graça Machel told them to come back later. She and Emma Bonino took me back to my hotel. They could see I was too emotional to continue.

The next day was the prize-giving ceremony. All of us had been asked to wear the traditional dress of our homelands, and a crowd gathered in the street to watch our procession. The Asturians were also wearing their pretty traditional clothes. For me it was as if the world had turned upside down. In my universe I'm nothing, a mere woman who works for wretched, imprisoned, penniless girls. Here I was being treated like a queen, a legendary creature.

All seven of us stepped forward, holding hands. There was the roar of applause again. Then we had to pay our respects to the Prince. I had been dreading this. I thought that meant that we would have to get down on our knees and bow our heads to the ground, like Cambodians have to do, to show we are mere dust beneath the feet of royalty.

I don't like to kneel. I'm no longer a slave. I hope I will never again have to abase myself and go down on my knees in front of anyone: I've done that much too much.

But the Prince arrived in front of me very simply, and said, 'Hello.' He held out his hand for me to shake. He talked to me naturally – he spoke in French. In Cambodia there is a special archaic language in which the king is addressed and no one speaks it outside the royal palace. But the Prince of Spain was friendly and he seemed genuinely interested.

Then I met his mother, Queen Sofia. She is a wonderful woman, firm and caring, and truly dedicated to the cause of helping women around the world. Emma Bonino translated for us. The Queen picked up Adana and played with her. Something about her was kind and good – I was drawn to her immediately.

I was fascinated by the casual charm of this amazing family. These people were the monarchs of a huge country and yet they behaved as though I was their equal. I was full of wonder. I felt that I had spoken from deep inside me. They knew what I had done, and what had been done to me, and yet they respected me anyway – a little Phnong girl, a dirty prostitute.

Afterwards we were asked to sign autographs, and there were photographers and a huge banquet. There was an enormous press of people. My feet were bleeding from the shoes I had bought specially for the occasion – I wasn't used to high heels – so I surreptitiously hid them in my bag. I spent the rest of the evening shaking hands, dazed and barefoot.

The warm welcome of the Spanish made me think for the first time that our campaign had found real support and would no longer have to go begging. Until then almost every time we'd gone to big Western aid donors for money we were looked at with cold superiority. The money came in dribs and drabs, never when they said it would and often less than we'd expected. But when I returned to Cambodia I had enough money with me to undertake something really significant – and, just as important, I felt people had understood what we were doing and how important it was to help us. I felt we were no longer alone. Until then, everything I had done had been spontaneous, instinctive, a little disorganised. Now I felt that AFESIP could begin to plan for the future.

After completing the Tom Dy Centre my first priority was to find a place where the children we had rescued could grow up. Some children simply could never be returned to their families – the risk that they would be sold again was too high. By now we were housing several children, some as young as seven or eight, whom we had rescued from brothels. These girls had suffered enormously; they needed care, they needed someone to talk to and trust and they needed to go to school. They needed to rebuild themselves as people and I didn't want to give them to an institutional orphanage where they would be rejected and mocked, or at best just fed and watered.

I thought the best thing for these girls would be to grow up somewhere outside Phnom Penh. Sometimes the pimps stood outside our shelter in Tuol Kok and threatened girls – its location was becoming known – and there was a lot of movement, with new inmates arriving and women leaving all the time. It was not a stable place to grow up. The idea came to me that I could buy some land in Thloc Chhroy, near my father's house, and make it into a children's centre. I had visited my father several times and the village was growing – prosperity was spreading there, too. The school was spacious. The forest was close. There were a lot of new people in Thloc Chhroy and the old ones were excessively nice to me now that I was a white man's wife and drove there from the city in a car.

I thought I would show those villagers that even if you have been a prostitute, even if your skin is dark, you can still be a good person. You can be clever and you can succeed. After the way they had treated me, I had made a good life for myself. I was helping others and they could do that too.

Above all, if I built a shelter in Thloc Chhroy it would be far enough from Phnom Penh that the children would be safe. They could grow up in a garden, straight and strong, and go to school.

With the money from the Prince of Asturias Prize, AFESIP bought a piece of land right by the village school in Thloc Chhroy. As a matter of fact, the land we bought was the same field where I had thrown a grenade and practised cleaning a gun in military training. All around it were rice-paddies and orchards. On it we built a spacious house on stilts. It has a fish pond and a chicken coop, and space to house a dozen weaving looms and sewing machines so the girls can learn a trade. I wanted it to be beautiful for them, too, and we planted flowers together. A seed is like a little girl: it can look small and worthless, but if you treat it well then it will grow to be beautiful.

There are sixty children living in that centre now.

Whenever we find underage children in the brothels we always ask them if they want to see their families again. They are sometimes very young, but they deserve to be heard, and we do sometimes reintegrate girls back into their families if their parents can be trusted. We need to be sure that they won't be re-sold and we follow up such cases with frequent visits. Sometimes it is enough to give the family a little money to start up a business.

But often the girls beg to stay on with us. I take them to Thloc Chhroy. They see the little girls their age, seven, eleven, thirteen, in their blue skirts and white shirts, happy together. They see the food: it is good home cooking and many of these girls are hungry. They see animals and flowers. They know that all the girls in our house have done the same things they have done, lived through the same life they did. They ask me, 'If I stay here for a week, and try to go to school, can I have a school uniform like the others?' I tell them yes, and at the end of the week they want to stay for ever. They can live with us but only until they grow up. Then, hard as it is to say goodbye to a child you have brought up – for whom you are her only family – it is time for those girls to leave too.

The children moved into that centre in 1999 and when that happened my heart lifted. I felt that I had finally done something right. They live there in an atmosphere of love and understanding, and they know they are safe. We have sixty children there now: we recently expanded the house again. The youngest is Ath, who is thirteen months old: we shouldn't, strictly speaking, have taken him in, but someone left him in the rubbish outside our centre in Phnom Penh when he was a few days old and the cook adopted him.

One of the girls living in our Thloc Chhroy house right now is Sry Mach. She was six years old when AFESIP rescued her from a brothel, along with her sister, Sry Mouch, who was nine. That was in early 2006. The raid took place in a town near the Thai border and the raid rescued about ten girls, and those two sisters were by far the youngest prostitutes on sale. We took all ten girls back to Phnom Penh with us, but those two I took with me, on my lap. They were much too frightened to talk: they didn't answer my questions, only ate fruit like savages when I stopped on the roadside to buy them some food and held each other like little animals. They reminded me of baby birds, with their mouths open only for food.

Younger girls are very likely to become infected with HIV and other diseases because of tearing. Sry Mach has Aids. She is very sick: she has had pneumonia and tuberculosis, and she has been in hospital several times. She does not want to leave us to go to a special Aids charity. She's receiving anti-retroviral treatment from Médecins Sans Frontières and she has never told me much about her story, only that a white man hurt her. The AFESIP psychologist says Sry Mach has put her trauma behind her and we should help it stay that way, so we don't ask questions.

Another six-year-old whom we rescued recently is

called Moteta. We found her, beaten black and blue, in a cage in a Tuol Kok brothel. Another prostitute, one of our 'peer educators', had alerted us. She was sold to the brothel by her mother and almost immediately afterwards the *meebon*'s business had begun going bad. The *meebon* called a fortune-teller, who said that Moteta brought an evil spirit and to get rid of it they would have to hurt her, to beat it out. They had already sold her virginity, of course, but they put Moteta in a cage and beat her all over.

With children this young, you don't ask questions. Moteta calls me 'Grandmother' and I tell her, 'Don't be frightened, I'll protect you.' I promise her that nobody will ever hurt her again. She's used to working all the time; she's always trying to wash everyone's clothes or clean the house at the Thloc Chhroy centre; she was in the brothel for so long that she called the *meebon* her mother. She's been with us for eighteen months.

Our oldest resident in Thloc Chhroy is Ma Li: she's nineteen, but she's lived with us ever since she was rescued, four years ago, and she doesn't feel ready to leave yet. She has her school certificate but she wanted to stay to teach weaving, and she's in charge of all the little girls now.

Setting up the AFESIP children's centre in Thloc Chhroy is the best thing I have ever done. Most of the girls who live there are between twelve and fifteen years old. They are so sweet to each other. The older girls call the smallest ones 'younger sister', and when new girls come in they help them as much as they can. We have a nurse and we look after them. They go to the village school in crisp school uniforms. They can talk to a psychologist, but some of these girls don't want to talk, and weaving is also a kind of therapy, a way of clearing your mind and making something beautiful.

They are good girls and look after the elderly in the village. They're always very respectful of adults and they're always top of the class. At first the villagers rejected them for what they'd done, because they were dirty. They called them whores. But they admire them now. They protect them from strangers. They tell me, 'Somaly, you bring up your girls so beautifully.'

I tell the children I love them; I say they are good. I tell them, 'It's up to you to show that, no matter what has happened to you, you are still clever and good and strong.'

I know the people who paid money to hurt these children. I know the clients. Some of them are tourists, but most are Cambodians. They are *tuktuk* drivers, cops, shopkeepers – ordinary men. The only difference in social class is the order in which they use the girls. The richest, the government officials and big businessmen, go first. In the end, when a girl costs only five thousand riel – just over a dollar – it is the turn of the poor. It's hard to say which is worse.

To me, few people are lower than the men who use prostitutes. They pay to rape women, teenagers and little girls. They use violence – they hit, slap, bite, like in the Thai porn videos that are on sale everywhere. It excites them to use power and see pain. Although some clients pretend to believe that they are somehow doing the girls a favour the reality is violence and rape. I spent a lot of time thinking about why, in Cambodia, people felt justified in treating women and children this way.

How do you get made into somebody so careless of other people? The attitude is everywhere. Cambodians have been traumatised by years of war and suffering. It has made many people completely egocentric, especially in the cities. If there's an accident in the road they won't stop and help. The idea is, if you stop someone may accuse you of having caused the accident and you'll be stuck with the bill. And it's true – people will do that.

To men, women are like servants. It has always been like that in Cambodia. Girls are taught only shame and ignorance about their bodies and men have their first sexual experience in brothels. Rape is the only thing they know.

I wanted to try to at least begin to change this mentality. In 1999 Emma Bonino managed to get us funds for a campaign to educate men. We went to the Ministry of Defence to explain why this was essential and we received the authorisation to go to police stations and military camps to give lectures. The first time I did it everyone said, 'What? You're going to talk to them about sex? Aren't you embarrassed and ashamed?' I was definitely embarrassed, but I didn't think anyone else would do it.

I took Mr Chheng, a social worker from AFESIP, with me. We started off by explaining how to protect yourself from catching Aids. The men were interested because they were scared: the epidemic was becoming enormous. We explained everything, starting from the very basics. With the help of a banana we even showed them how to put on a condom. This was the moment to say things loud and clear, to get them talking. By asking questions we arrived at the problem of their relationship with their wives.

A lot of Cambodian men say they go to brothels because their wives don't like making love. They talk about this openly. Cambodian women are taught to submit; there's not much female pleasure in our culture. The men say their wives' passivity ends up disgusting them. No one is happy in this situation. Tradition, when it says anything, says the wife must stay quiet, unmoving, while the husband gets on with his business.

One man said his wife actually told him to go to prostitutes. He never saw her naked and never even saw her breast when she breastfed their children. If he tried to take off her clothes she said, 'If you want to do it like in those films, go see the whores.' He burst out laughing: 'Oh, those young Vietnamese girls, just freshly arrived – when they get undressed, what a marvel! They're plump, they have white skin like young piglets!'

The AFESIP lecturers like Mr Chheng, as well as the women, confronted these subjects simply and straightforwardly. We talked about mutual pleasure, and pain. We showed them a video of a little girl who recounted how she had been raped – exactly what had happened to her and who had done it. Sometimes one or two of the girls from our shelter would talk about what had been done to them. Often the men in the audience would break down and cry. Many of them had been clients of prostitutes just like her, but somehow it had never occurred to them to think about how they were being treated.

In the first month we received four hundred letters from men who had attended our lectures. In the two years that we did this we reached thousands of men; most of them were soldiers and policemen, men who really needed to think about these things. We were teaching them about what the brothels are really like and how they work. It was also useful because we made a few friends in police stations, even though they usually weren't very important officers.

But it took enormous amounts of organisation and energy getting the public to come, touring the education team and maintaining the cars on our terrible roads. And in 2000, after Emma Bonino resigned from her job with the European Union, our funding from ECHO stopped. We decided to wait for better days to start the programme up again.

At that time we were suddenly swamped by a huge arrival of girls from two rescue operations. Almost all of them asked to stay on at the shelter. It was a bad time to be short of funds. We called a meeting of all AFESIP Cambodia personnel to work out what needed to be done. In the end we all had to pool our salaries in order to feed the girls.

AFESIP's financial problems always come at the end of the year. Whatever number of girls we predict will come, there are always more. It's impossible to refuse them shelter or to evict them. I could receive funding for five hundred girls: there would still be more. The money is never enough, and at the end of the year we almost always run out.

13

AFESIP

The year 2000 was a difficult time for us as a family. At around the same time that AFESIP lost the European funding for our educational campaign I had a miscarriage. This was very painful to me. I felt horribly guilty that I had not been more careful and rested as the doctors said I should. Also, Sophanna's husband left her for another woman. He took off with all her savings. She was still a volunteer with us, teaching sewing classes for free, but she had a part-time job with PADEK, also teaching sewing.

AFESIP took shape slowly, in fits and starts: it was never a planned progression. We grew as the need became obvious. We set up basic classes in reading and writing Khmer. We expanded our training programmes to teach cooking, weaving and hairdressing – skills that can quickly translate into jobs. We began teaching every one of our residents small business skills, things like how to keep accounts and run a shop. Whatever they end up doing it'll be important that they learn to keep their own accounts.

Father began coming to the centre more often. He had moved to Phnom Penh to be with Mother. She was still the cook and caretaker of our shelter, and Father volunteered to teach the girls to read and write.

It amused me to overhear him teaching girls the *chbap srey*. He would assemble them in a circle under the shade of a tree and after class he would tell them that the good parts of the old code are the need for silence and privacy. It doesn't mean you should not defend yourself. That, he said, you are permitted to do.

Father never spoke to the girls directly about prostitution. But he told them, 'What you have learned from experience is worth much more than gold. If you have a house it may burn down. Any kind of possession can be lost but your experience is yours for ever. Keep it and find a way to use it.'

We had begun receiving funding from UNICEF, from the Dutch network SKN and from the Spanish government and the agency Manos Unidas. Our Tom Dy Centre grew larger. The sex business in Cambodia was becoming more and more professional and it was taking on a new market.

The temples of Angkor Wat were drawing tourists.

172

Every night of the year thousands of foreigners rented hotel rooms in the nearby town of Siem Reap. They were Japanese, German, American, Australian – and some of them, apparently, wanted to sleep with children. We began finding so many girls imprisoned in brothels in Siem Reap that in 2001 we opened a shelter there too. Until we intervened the police had never done anything about it because they had never been told to.

Most of the clients of Cambodian prostitutes are locals, but some are foreigners. The sale of sex is a very profitable business. The traffickers earn a lot of money, especially if the girl is young. In Siem Reap an ordinary girl, not a virgin, might bring in about fifteen dollars per client. Let's say five a day. Four girls will make you almost ten thousand dollars a month and cost you nothing but a bit of rice and a few guns. With profits like these it's clear that you can bribe whomever you want.

And it's not just Cambodia, by any means. Every day fresh girls are trucked from Cambodia across the Thai border. Cambodian girls go to Thailand, Vietnamese girls come to Cambodia: Cambodia is a destination country, a transit zone, a place of export. It's an industry, whose product is young human flesh. With fake passports the girls are sent on to Taiwan, Malaysia, Canada. Trafficking of women by mafias around the world is a huge global business, worth as much money as drugs, and one of its great centres is South-East Asia.

In 2002 I was in France, accepting an award from the town of Nantes, when I received a phone call. A group of policeman had come to the AFESIP shelter in Phnom Penh, armed. We had recently taken in fourteen young Vietnamese girls after a raid on a brothel. The girls had been brought to Cambodia from Vietnam and they had no passports. The police arrested the girls for 'immigration irregularities'. They took them away.

Of course, what really must have happened was that the pimps paid a lot of money to the judge to get the girls back. Young Vietnamese girls are a prize in Cambodia: their skin is so white and fresh. By the time we got a court order to release them most of the girls had already disappeared; we never saw them again. One girl who was still in prison was pregnant after being raped by the prison guards.

If I had been there, if I had had a gun on me, I don't know what I might have done. I felt real violence. There is no law, no police, no justice to protect little worms like us. If you're strong, or if you have powerful protectors, you're left alone. If not, forget it.

After that happened we set up an AFESIP office in Vietnam and began talking to the Vietnamese and Cambodian authorities about setting up a safe way to get these girls home. We proposed that the Cambodian police could release the girls into the care of AFESIP, at least until the Vietnamese authorities could identify them. That would keep the girls safe. We pointed out that we could help the police by identifying the people who created the problem – the traffickers. We also suggested that AFESIP could build a training centre in Vietnam, like the Tom Dy Centre in Phnom Penh.

The authorities agreed and we made new, separate arrangements for the Vietnamese girls we found. We rented another short-term shelter where they could stay: some of them spent only three months with us waiting for their papers, though for others it was much longer. We asked an ethnic Vietnamese woman from Cambodia to give them literacy classes and a Vietnamese-speaking former prostitute gave them counselling.

We also set up a new organisation, AFESIP Vietnam, and opened a shelter in Ho Chi Minh City. It works just as we do in Phnom Penh. Some girls have nowhere to go: they are homeless or have violent families. Often they have stepfathers who try to take advantage of them; almost always, there is rejection by their family or community. In almost every province nowadays there are traders – people who make a commission from the brothels when they bring in a new girl. It is sometimes better to stay out of harm's way and learn a skill.

In 2001 I became pregnant again and the doctor said the baby was a boy. Ning was eleven and Adana six, and they were both ecstatic to be having a baby brother. I tried to take better care of myself: I tried to travel less along the bumpy roads and tracks between provincial villages, and to stay in Phnom Penh a little more.

Nikolai was born in April 2002. The girls were adorable. They stayed with me in the hospital room in Bangkok that night, along with their new brother, and every time he whimpered they raced over to his cot to tell him, 'Hush, little brother,' all night long.

By this time AFESIP's operation in Cambodia had become much more professional. We had set up teams of social workers, many of them former prostitutes, to go out every day distributing condoms, telling girls how to get to our shelter and advising them on how to calm clients who are drunk or violent. They also collected information on where the brothels were. We printed flyers with our phone number. We created and expanded an AFESIP clinic where women could come in every day for free medical treatment.

We also offered small sums of money to informers, whom we call peer educators. Often these are former prostitutes who alert us when a girl is very sick, or when a minor arrives in the brothels from the countryside. Nowadays pimps change their 'personnel' every two or three months in order to attract customers with the appeal of novelty. They sell the girls on, afterwards, to brothels in the countryside or in Thailand.

We hired a psychologist to talk with the girls because so many of them are depressed and suicidal. We sent teams out at night to the parks and open areas where some of the worst kinds of prostitution take place. The 'orange women' are girls who sell oranges in the public gardens: for the price of an orange the client also fondles the girl. For twenty-five cents he can have sex with her. Often a crowd of men will gang-rape an orange girl, and a dead body in the morning is not uncommon.

These prostitutes don't have the money to pay for medical care, but they have our telephone number. They call us when they're ill, and our *tuktuk* driver brings them to the clinic. Here they can receive treatment and rest for fifteen days or so, if they are able to do this. We make use of the time to explain that there are ways out of their situation; their lives aren't over. When they understand this hope can return to them: they may begin to believe that they are not alone, that we can help. One day they will come to us; until then they help us by letting us know about children and young girls who are being held against their will.

We cannot rescue every prostitute in every brothel. We try to focus on the worst cases, the captives, the children. When we hear about these things we send investigators to the neighbourhood: one of our full-time investigators is Srieng, the young cop I met when I first moved to Phnom Penh. They pose as clients. They talk to the girls in the brothels and take down their statements. If the girls say they have been sold we make up a dossier and take it to the government office of trafficking for evaluation so that they can decide what needs to be done and verify all the details.

The local police are called in but we try to withhold the exact location of the brothel until the last possible minute. AFESIP usually goes along on the raid to observe the proceedings. We shelter the girls at the AFESIP centre, for at least a few days, while a case can be prepared against the pimps.

I talk with every woman who comes into our centre. I don't judge her and she knows that. I sit beside her and explain that if you've been a prostitute it doesn't mean your life is over. I talk about the women we employ, many of whom are former prostitutes too, and everything they have done with their lives. I show her my clothes and say, 'You can learn to make this.' I tell her, 'Don't trust me, because you mustn't trust people. Decide for yourself.'

In 2003 we opened an AFESIP garment workshop, and I take the women there. They know that in Cambodia a garment factory is often a brutal place, crowded and poorly ventilated. Many women are so ill-treated and exploited there that they may even choose to become prostitutes voluntarily, though initially they don't usually realise what that means. Our AFESIP Fair Fashion workshop isn't like that: it's a decent environment where every employee is treated like a human, and each girl knows that every woman has gone through the same kind of pain as her.

She can see for herself. It is possible to get out of prostitution and make your way to a decent life that is clean, where you are treated like a human being. Almost all the women who come to us have some kind of illness or another. Sometimes it's just that they're starved and beaten but – ten or fifteen unprotected sex acts every day – you catch diseases. Many of them have tuberculosis or HIV, and they usually agree to stay with AFESIP, if only to rest for a few days.

If they leave, these women know they can come back. There's a wall around our shelter in Phnom Penh, but that's to keep the pimps out, not to keep the girls in. And if they stay with us we give them a completely new environment. At the Tom Dy Centre a paralegal gives each woman advice and explains their rights. They usually have no idea about this – after all, there is nothing in daily life in Cambodia to indicate that they have any. The paralegal urges them to lodge a complaint with the police. This can be very important so they can rebuild themselves. These girls need to feel they are not bad, that they are not guilty for what they have done.

If they want to talk this helps to free them of the burden of their oppression. We have a Khmer psychologist on the staff for this reason. But talking is not an easy or common thing in Cambodia. People tend to be very restrained and tradition demands you remain silent about misfortune. Only old women, who are freed of all familial responsibility, can sometimes speak out and talk about their hardships together. They take it in turn, according to rank, but no one talks back.

In 2003 we opened an AFESIP office in Thailand, where the prostitution and trafficking industry was even larger than in Cambodia. We began looking through the centres where the Thai authorities kept illegal immigrants: many girls in there were from Cambodia and Vietnam and had been taken across the border by force to become prostitutes. The centres were not safe for them, and we began helping them get back home safely. We also began participating in rescue operations in Thailand.

In 2006 we set up another office in Laos, with a shelter and training centre in Sisattanak Province. A few years ago a survey by the International Labour Organization found that almost one in ten women and girls from Sisattanak had left home to go to Thailand. One-third of them were under twenty-five. These girls leave home with a trader, often a woman who tells them they will be hired as domestic servants. They become bodies on sale in the big glassed-in bars in Bangkok where the world's tourists pick a girl by her number, or they service locals in other, much dirtier and more violent places at the side of the road.

AFESIP's shelter in Laos gives them medical care and vocational training so that they can return to their villages or start a new life on their own. We teach the women to cultivate mulberry trees and to produce and market silk. There are so many that soon we'll need another shelter in Savannakhet Province. Eventually we need to start a shelter in Burma, too, though it's difficult to get the authorities there to agree: we see huge numbers of Burmese girls.

At Siem Reap there's a brothel with Korean, Romanian and, especially, Moldavian women. The Asian clientele will pay a great deal for that kind of exoticism. It's a global industry and for some reason the world puts up with it.

The advantage of this network of offices is that AFESIP can now help the authorities of all these countries to fight trafficking together. We can act as a mediator between Vietnam, Laos, Cambodia, Thailand, Malaysia and Singapore, to help them pool their efforts to protect these women and to help them return to their homes. Most important, we can give them information so they can fight the traffickers.

In the years since we first set up AFESIP in Cambodia, we have helped about three thousand victims of prostitution get back on their feet. In Thailand, Laos and Vietnam we have helped another thousand or so. All of them have to go back to normal life at some point, and they have to be equipped to look after themselves.

Reintegration can be a long process. It takes a year and a half to train a woman to take the government's hairdressing certificate. If she has been badly damaged it may take months for her to rebuild herself, before she is ready even to begin. Some girls can become independent after ten months. For others, who have suffered deeper trauma, it takes over two years.

When their training is over we find every girl a job in an environment that is safe and humane, or we buy her the basics to set up an independent life – a sewing machine or a pig. In the NGO world I've learned that this is called 'micro credit'. We also visit her regularly, at least once a month for the first three months and repeatedly after that, for at least three years. That's the minimum time for assuring ourselves that the enterprise has succeeded.

Some of the girls are like part of our family. They invite us to their weddings; after ten years, they still bring us their children for a visit.

We can do all this only because governments and organisations give us money, but we also need the donors' support in much more important ways. To explain this, we always ask our benefactors to come and visit AFESIP. A few years ago the Spanish Secretary of State for Foreign Affairs, Mr Cortes, came to see us with a government delegation. They visited the sites. Mr Cortes listened through an interpreter while a few of the girls told their stories. He came away transformed. He told me that he had heard me explain the work several times in Spain and that he had read the reports, but what he had heard here directly from the lips of the victims surpassed understanding. He was overwhelmed.

Sometimes it's hard to convince the donors to visit. They stay in their air-conditioned offices, push their paperwork around and simply haven't the time. I try to tell them that, to the girls, their human presence and moral support is as important as their financial aid. They need to be recognised as full fellow beings.

We have a great deal of support from many people around the world, and for that we are very grateful. But we sometimes have the impression that for the benefactors giving money is a way of getting rid of the problem – they don't want to hear any more about it. But it goes without saying that we can't do this work alone. It's too big for us. We want our action to be part of a whole chain of action, because it is not enough to look after some of the victims: we want the traffic in women to end.

14

The Victims

Since we started AFESIP the brothels have grown larger
and more violent. We find women chained to sewers.
Girls have come to us beaten half to death. They are so
young. Increasingly we see that the pimps have addicted
them to drugs so that they won't ever try to escape.
When I was young we were terrorised with snakes and
heavy fists, but these girls suffer electric shocks and tortures. They have marks that are much worse than
anything I have ever borne.

One day a girl called Srey Mom arrived at the shelter
in Phnom Penh. She was bleeding and black and blue all
over. I knew we should take her to the hospital, because
I thought she might die from the wounds, but she begged
us not to take her there – she said the pimps would go

there to look for her. She pleaded, 'If I die, let me die here.'

We looked after her. When she got better we started to talk. She was fifteen. She had been sold to a brothel run by a well-known pimp, mainly for the military police. This man is known to have killed several girls. Srey Mom was locked up there for four months, beaten, chained, raped without respite. The house, which was in Tuol Kok, was built on stilts above a marsh like so many Cambodian houses. The toilets gave out directly into the water.

Srey Mom made a hole in the floor big enough to slip through and that evening she waded through the watery filth. She went to the police and told them everything. The police wrote down everything she said in a correct manner. Then they proposed that they take her to a shelter on a motorcycle. She gladly accepted. In fact, they took her back to the brothel from where she had escaped.

The pimps thrashed her, and she thought they would kill her for sure. She made it out again, through the same hole, which was hidden. In the morning, having asked some people the way, she arrived at the AFESIP shelter, which wasn't far off. She didn't want to go out because she was certain the pimps, and their friends the police, would be patrolling the area. She didn't even trust the hospital – she knew that anyone could just sell her on for a few dollars.

Srey Mom said one girl in her brothel was kept chained up. She said another girl had been tied up and burned because she refused clients and had tried to escape. Srey was certain she was destined for the same fate. And her grandmother sold her into this.

Often, it must be said, the family doesn't know where their daughters are heading. I think some parents truly believe that when they sell their daughters to traders, these men and women will find them domestic work as maids in the big city. But most of them do know their children are going into prostitution. To avoid commissions they take their daughters to the brothels themselves. They know they are heading into the huge prostitution networks that fan all over Cambodia. But these parents do it anyway. They care about nothing except themselves.

Sokhane was the first child we had who died of Aids. Her parents died when she was seven years old and her older sister sold her into domestic service in Phnom Penh. The wife beat her and the husband raped her, and one morning when she was about eight she left the house where she was working and walked as far as she could.

Sokhane ended up in the gardens in front of the Royal Palace, where a *motodup* driver started talking to her. He told her he would help her and took her to a brothel in Tuol Pak where she was sold, and raped, and tortured.

When we rescued her she was twelve. She had tuberculosis, along with Aids, and was so close to death that her pimp had just dumped her at the hospital. The hospital called us, because if they were going to treat her someone was going to have to pay. I went there and we found the money to pay for her care. She had every kind of mark on her body; she was so thin she seemed made of rope. She looked like me and her situation felt exactly like the one I had once been in. Everyone was frightened to touch her but I took her in my arms. I couldn't help it.

I suppose some man paid a lot of money to have sex with Sokhane so he could purify himself of the Aids infection. Many men believe you can eliminate Aids if you have sex with a virgin child. This belief is an abomination and responsible for enormous, terrible suffering: a small child is even more likely to catch Aids than the older girls, because of tearing.

Sokhane got better for a little while. She used to love her blue and white school uniform, but she knew she was going to die. That affected me enormously and I spent a lot of time with her. She used to ask me whether there was a God and why he allowed such things to happen to a little girl who had never done anything wrong.

The first thing she asked me was to find and look after her little brother. We took him to a Buddhist pagoda: that was when I began asking a group of bonzes to look after the younger brothers of our girls and bring them up at the temple. We can't house boys in our shelters.

Sokhane was very disturbed. One night, when she was already very sick, she asked me to sleep next to her. In the middle of the night, while I was sleeping, she cut my foot with a knife. She said she wanted to mix our blood – she rubbed her bleeding arm on me. She knew that could endanger me and I think that she did it so she wouldn't be alone in her suffering. It's hard to say what goes through another person's head.

Kolap was six years old when her mother sold her. When they got to the brothel Kolap thought her job was only going to be doing the washing-up, but she pleaded with her mother not to leave her. She hugged her mother by the neck and her mother slapped her and pushed her away. When Kolap grabbed her ankles her mother kicked her. She walked away with fifty dollars and Kolap's virginity was sold.

They scrubbed her down and plastered her with a lightening cream in order to make her a more appealing colour. Since she resisted they beat her for several days in succession. After her first week they sewed her up again, without an anaesthetic, and sold her to another brothel. She went from one brothel to another until she was ten, when we rescued her. Her life during those years was truly a journey through hell.

About a year after she came to us, Kolap asked me if I would take her to see her mother in Kon Dal. Before that she had always refused. I took her to her home village to find her mother. The woman actually started to cry when she saw her.

Kolap said, 'Don't cry. I've come to ask you, why did you sell me? Why did you hit me when I kissed you? Why did you kick me when I tried to hold on to you? You had fifty dollars in your hands.'

'I didn't sell you,' stammered the woman. 'I didn't know it was a brothel.'

'How can you say that?'

'We had nothing to eat.'

'You're lying. You've managed to live pretty well till now.'

Kolap's little brother intervened to say he feared she would sell their younger sister too, only the child was handicapped and nobody wanted to buy her.

'You haven't changed. But you're no longer my mother. That's my mother,' said Kolap, and pointed at me. 'She didn't give birth to me but she has given me all the rest.'

We left. Kolap didn't want to stay for another minute in that house of sorrows. She was eleven years old, with the body of a child, but her spirit was weighed down by an adult suffering.

Kolap is fourteen now and she lives in our children's centre in Thloc Chhroy. She's tall and she's top of her class in secondary school, and she has never spoken of her mother again. She only says that as soon as she leaves us she will bring her brother and sister to live with her and send them to school.

Sometimes parents take us to court to get their daughters back, with an eye to selling them on again. There's a profit to be made. But our legal position is strong. A mother who sells her daughter disqualifies herself, and our statute authorises us to shelter and represent such children.

*

From time to time I am engulfed by rage at what I see around me. Recently there was the case of one young girl, Kaseng. Her parents were out one evening and she was wandering in the streets when she was captured by a group of six or seven drunken men in their fifties. She was eight. They took her to a house and raped her one by one. Since she was too narrow they took a knife and cut her vagina. Someone brought her to us. I took the child to hospital to get her sewn up, and to the police to make a report. She began to recover. Her mother, who was very poor, refused to take her back. She said ever since the child had been born she had brought nothing but bad luck.

When the trial came up, I couldn't go, but another AFESIP staff-member was there. The rapists had paid off the judge. They claimed that Kaseng was provocatively dressed and that they'd paid her. In any case, they said, she was young and would have time to remake her life. The judge determined that it was impossible to send men of such venerable age to prison and they got off scot-free.

This child was a victim in every way: of the men, of the courts, of her family. We could have appealed the case. But she didn't want to – she pleaded with me not to do it. 'I don't want to see them or hear what they're saying about me,' she begged. 'I never want to go to court again.'

Blind with anger, I lashed out. I told everything to a close adviser of the Prime Minister, a man who had helped me in other circumstances. I asked him to tell me how such denial of justice could be possible in a country that claims to be civilised. How can we allow our justice system to remain so corrupted by organised crime, and by ordinary bribery, that a case as vile as this one goes unpunished?

My friend looked into it and referred the matter back to the court. We're still waiting to find out if Kaseng can get some kind of compensation. But this can't work for every case – I can't telephone people in high places every time we lose in court, because sometimes it happens several times a month.

Even if we do make a scandal, the political authorities can only try to force the judicial machine into action. Then things get slowed down and nothing happens. The results are rarely satisfactory. We have laws in Cambodia, but everyone ignores them. Instead, what prevails is the law of money. With money you can buy a judge, a policeman – whatever you want. There are moments when I want to throw in the towel in and stop doing this. I feel it is too big for me to fight all this – the pimps, the corruption, the judges who aren't for sale, but only because they were bought long ago.

Corruption is like a gangrene at the heart of the Cambodian police and legal systems. All too often, justice is for sale. In the beginning, even when AFESIP managed to pressure the police into conducting a raid on a brothel, the pimps were often freed within days.

Since the start of AFESIP, we've brought about two thousand cases before the courts. We've won only about

5 per cent of them, and most of those victories have been recent. We know our way around the system better now and I think the judges are more careful these days: they know that AFESIP doesn't give up easily. Still, it's rare for the criminals to spend more than six months in prison and most of them continue to be freed after just a few days in police custody.

Maybe it was different in Cambodia before Pol Pot. Even today you do find good people in the countryside – villagers who care for each other and are always ready to share their meal with a stranger. But I was born after the great dislocations that ripped apart my country and as soon as I opened my eyes on the world I saw only violence and corruption. Where are the supposedly admirable traditions of the Khmers? Where is their Buddhist morality?

I'm a Buddhist – just an ordinary Buddhist. I go to the temple sometimes; I give rice to feed the elderly at the village temple in Thloc Chhroy. But the men who torture girls also go to the temple. Are they Buddhists?

One day I put this question to the priest who heads the temple I go to. He said, 'Somaly, after thirty years of war we even have monks who go to brothels and rape children. And there are others who are good and don't know why they're good.'

I've spent a decade building AFESIP, and it's been a decade of pain. I can't distance myself from the suffering of these girls. We carry the same wounds. I share their suffering, their horrors. It is difficult for me not to blame all men for the actions of a few.

Sometimes, in those years, Pierre had a lot to put up with. Our marriage was under a lot of strain and it seemed not even the birth of our darling Nikolai could bring us closer together. In 2004 we separated, and we are now divorced.

In 2004 AFESIP began receiving reports about a hotel, the Chai Hour II. It was one of the biggest new brothels in Phnom Penh, a six-floor supermarket of female flesh where customers could pick out girls standing behind a glass box and have them delivered straight to their hotel room. Our investigators talked with girls who worked there and they said they had been forced into prostitution. Of the roughly two hundred girls working in the hotel as 'hostesses' and 'karaoke girls', many were minors. There were also virgins for sale on the premises.

To free these girls we had no choice but to go to the police. We knew this wouldn't necessarily mean the guilty would be punished.

And the Chai Hour II was a big operation – by far the largest brothel that we had ever taken on. We knew that it was run by wealthy and powerful traffickers, and we realised that they probably had close connections with police and government officials.

Our dossier on the hotel was in the hands of the authorities by September. At the beginning of December the police agreed to conduct a raid. An investigating magistrate had been designated as the person in charge. Once everything was decided we had to move fast, since leaks were bound to occur.

The raid took place on the afternoon of 7 December 2004. Some of the people at the hotel managed to flee, but eight pimps were arrested, along with eighty-three women and girls. There weren't enough police cells to house the girls and many of them were underage. AFESIP agreed to take them into the shelter that night, to keep them safe while the police needed them for questioning. Several of the girls had agreed to bring charges.

I spoke to each of the girls. Some of them said they wanted to go back to work. One or two were the mistresses of highly placed men. For a man of high position there's almost an obligation to keep a little virgin or a minor in a luxurious brothel – it's a mark of status. (They usually also have wives, and 'official' mistresses with their own apartments.) These girls had expensive mobile phones, and used them to ring their protectors in a tone of outrage. I explained to them that AFESIP doesn't keep women against their will, but they were with us under police authority. The police required them to be available for questioning for a few days: then they could leave.

Most of the girls were in shock. Several showed marks of their beatings. The youngest ones, especially, found it hard to comprehend that they were now in safety – that, if they wanted to, they could stay with us and go to school.

When I left the AFESIP shelter that night a large black Lexus was parked outside. Two men – two pimps – said they wanted to come in. We refused. Our rules forbid the traffickers from coming on to our premises: that's why our Phnom Penh centre has a high wall and a strong gate.

The next morning I began receiving phone calls. Well-placed friends called me, warning me to be cautious – 'Somaly, you're dealing with important people here. You're going to get into trouble.' The assistant of a person who worked with us in the anti-trafficking unit of the Ministry of the Interior called me in tears to say that her boss was in the office of the police chief, being fired.

I called another person I knew, and he said that he'd heard that the eight pimps had all been released. He too warned me that I should be careful. He told me, 'Stay out of this, it's too big for you.' He told me I should free all the women from the Chai Hour II.

Then a woman who worked at the AFESIP shelter phoned to tell me that a mob of men was forming in front of the gates. She said that some of them were in uniform, from both the military and the police. What were they to do?

At 11.40 my contact at the Interior Ministry finally called me back. He said, 'Release the girls. Your life is in danger. We have no power over this.'

At around noon, while I was still on the phone, about thirty armed men smashed down the gates. The girls, and the AFESIP staff inside, were terrified. They recognised some of the attackers as the eight men who had just been freed from jail. The men forced all the girls they could find into cars or on to motorcycles that were waiting outside. Their ringleader hit the staff and threatened to kill them.

When they left, they took all the women and girls they could find in our centre away. There were ninety-one girls, some of whom had been with us for just a few weeks, who were beginning to smile and to trust that we could keep them safe. We never saw any of them again.

One girl hid in the toilets the whole time. When I got to the AFESIP shelter, and took her in my arms, she couldn't stop sobbing and shaking.

I was angry, so horribly angry. What can you do, when the mafias that run the trade in women become so rich that they are more powerful than the law?

I phoned Pierre, who was in Laos. He phoned the French embassy. A staff-member from the AFESIP shelter called: she said she had heard a group of boys in the market saying they were going to lob grenades into the centre and kill the staff one by one. I called a meeting and told everyone we had to suspend our operations temporarily, and gave them all time off. I tried to help them stay calm, but I was frightened too.

I'm not an intellectual. I have no specific field. I don't know how to speak properly and I've never had a proper education. But sometimes it's up to me to stay calm, to have an answer for everyone, to give people strength and help them to overcome themselves. I live day by day, hour by hour, minute by minute. I don't know what will happen to me when I leave this room: nobody does.

The next day, 9 December, some of the local press began reporting that the girls from the Chai Hour II had pushed down the gate in an attempt to escape because

AFESIP was holding them against their will. They also reported that all the girls were over eighteen. I began receiving I don't know how many calls from people of influence in government and the police suggesting that I just keep quiet, that I not interfere in what didn't concern me. Friends warned me that I would get myself killed if I tried to make this into a confrontation and suggested I leave the country for a while.

The municipal chief of police produced a communiqué that charged us with kidnapping the women. We had impeded the liberty of working people. It was a statement full of venom. Journalists from local newspapers reported that the Chai Hour II was an ordinary hotel, offering massages and a karaoke parlour, and that all the girls were willing to testify that they were not prostitutes.

Pierre was flying home to Cambodia but he called a press conference en route, in Bangkok, to try to get support for us from the international press.

The next day my children were followed by motorcycles on their way home from school. I knew I had to go to Kampong Cham to check on the children in Thloc Chhroy. The staff who worked there were terrified that there would be a raid on them too and the children were in a state of panic.

We left at four in the morning, but still a car followed us. They weren't very clever – we managed to lose them before we reached Thloc Chhroy. I tried to calm the girls. I told them nothing would happen to anyone and that we had lawyers. I was trying to think clearly but I was frightened. I didn't want to take my friends' advice and leave the country – I couldn't simply get up and leave all these girls, and AFESIP's staff, behind.

But it seemed that pressure was also building from an unexpected corner. Officials from the American embassy came to see me, to find out what was going on and to look into it themselves. We began receiving phone calls from people at the UN. I was invited to the French embassy to speak with the Ambassador. Journalists began to call.

In the space of a few days the tide began to turn. In Europe newspapers were reporting the case and we heard that diplomats from the European Union and the US government were threatening Cambodia with economic sanctions if more was not done to stop sexual trafficking and corruption in the government. The Chai Hour II was now a symbol of something greater.

The English-language *Cambodia Daily* led an investigation to see who had forced open the gates of the AFESIP shelter. Neighbours testified that it was the traffickers themselves who had led the assault. AFESIP received discreet invitations to return to work, and the government agreed to set up a panel to investigate the case and look into whether any corruption was involved.

Many months later, the commission reported that it 'lacked evidence' of any corruption or that any women had been forcibly removed from the shelter. You see, some people are too big to take on. If I spelled out names there'd be a bullet through my head tomorrow: I'd have scaled the boundary between what separates life and death in our country. That still may happen, one day. But, before it does, at least I will have spoken out.

In some ways, the Chai Hour II case unblocked the system for us. AFESIP began receiving markedly more help from the authorities. But eighteen months later the Chai Hour II case came back to haunt us in the most horrible, personal way possible.

In July 2006, while the journalist Mariane Pearl was in Phnom Penh to interview me for *Glamour* magazine, Ning's school phoned me: Ning had disappeared. She had left the school grounds at midday and hadn't come back. The mobile phone I'd given her for her fourteenth birthday wasn't picking up. I panicked. Ning is not the kind of girl who would just take off. She is a sweet, loving child: she has her own secrets, but she would never seek to worry me.

No, my instant reaction was that my deepest fear had been realised. The traffickers had taken my child. In Cambodia this is not a far-fetched scenario. Every year thousands of girls are abducted and sold into prostitution. Most of them are poor, but my adopted daughter would be a special target. My blood iced.

I phoned Pierre. He and I had recently taken the decision to separate and he was temporarily in Thailand. He promised to fly to Cambodia right away. Then I phoned everyone I knew in the police and in the government and told them what had happened. And I settled down to focus on finding Ning.

This is what I know how to do – I know how to trace

girls through the prostitution networks. Every investigator we had ever employed at AFESIP went to see every informant who had ever contacted us. Very quickly we heard that Ning had been seen getting into a car with several people in it just outside her school. In the car was a woman and several men, and the woman was recognised as someone connected to the Chai Hour II.

Four days went by, of frantic phone calls and the even worse terror of waiting. During those days Mariane was a rock for me. She told me about the abduction of her own husband, Daniel Pearl, by Islamic militants in Pakistan in 2002. She helped me retain control.

I knew that if Ning had already been taken to Thailand we might lose her. The first thing we did was send people out to the main border towns with her photo. Our only hope was if she was still in the country. In that case, we might still find her and get her back.

Working closely with the police and the authorities we finally tracked Ning down. She was in Battambang. She was in the hands of traffickers, and along with them was a boy she knew. He had persuaded her that he was going to commit suicide over her and she had felt pity for him so she had left the school to talk. He had led my daughter to a car full of armed men.

The people involved have been released from jail, although the trial is still pending. The Chai Hour II is still in business, still a brothel – it's called the Leang Hour. And the woman in the car has never been found.

Conclusion

Today in our children's shelter in Kampong Cham Province we have a twelve-year-old girl with deep circular scars around her neck and upper arms from the time a drunken client tried to hurt her. One charming fourteen-year-old girl who has been living with us for almost a year has lost her mind. When we found her she was locked in the basement of a brothel and for the first few months she was mute and couldn't control her body. Now she speaks and she's learning to help out in the kitchen – she's very sweet, like a small child, but she doesn't always make sense. She wasn't always this way: she can read and write Khmer. We're still not sure who she is.

Sometimes I am flooded with anger at what these children have been through. I speak with some of the girls and I find myself overcome by having shared in their suffering. It eats away at my bones and guts until I feel almost deranged.

Conclusion

How do you get to be this way? Three decades of bombing, genocide, starvation and now my country is in a state of moral bankruptcy. The Khmers no longer know who they are, what their identity is.

During the Khmer Rouge regime people detached themselves from any kind of human feeling, because feeling meant pain. They learned not to trust their neighbours, their family, their own children. To avoid going mad they shrank to the smallest part of a human, which is 'me'. After the regime fell they were silent, either because they had helped cause the suffering or because this is what they had learned to do in order to survive.

The Khmer Rouge eliminated everything that mattered to Cambodians. And after they fell people no longer cared for anything except for money. I suppose they want to give themselves some insurance in case of another catastrophe, even though the lesson of Pol Pot, if there is one, is that there can be no insurance against catastrophe.

More than half the people in Cambodia today were born after the fall of the Khmer Rouge. Things should be improving. But the country is in a state of chaos where the only rule is every man for himself. The people in power don't always work for the common good. When I was young we were poorer, but school was free in those days. Today school has to be paid for and you can buy a diploma – or get one for free if you show your teacher a gun. The justice system is for sale and mafias are close to power: the prostitution business is worth $500 million a year, almost as much as the annual budget of the government.

Cambodian people have always been trained to be obedient, and they have always been poor. In Cambodia, one child in eight dies before the age of five. The streets are full of rubbish and flies and shit, and the rain churns it into muck. More than a third of the population lives on less than a dollar a day, and you have to pay the hospital when you get sick.

Men have the power. Not all the time: in front of their parents they keep quiet. With the powerful, they too must stay silent and perhaps prostrate themselves. But once these encounters are over they go home to assume the upper hand and give orders. If their wife resists they hit her.

There is one law for women: silence before rape and silence after. We're taught when we're little to be like the silk cotton tree: *dam kor*. Deaf and dumb. Blind too, if possible. It's normal to beat girls. To many people they're a kind of cattle. Your daughters will look after you because that's their duty. Other than that, they're not worth much.

One-third of the prostitutes in Phnom Penh are young children. These girls are sold, and beaten and abused for some kind of pleasure. In the end I don't think there is any way you can explain or justify that, or the homeless children scrounging through rubbish, inhaling glue from little cans you can buy for five hundred riel from every hardware stall, or the stolen children who are trucked into Thailand for the modern slave trade. Trying to explain it is not what I do. I keep my head down and try to help one girl after another. It is a big enough task.

I still feel dirty, or that I carry bad luck around with me. When I sleep my dreams are filled with violence and rape. Mostly they're nightmares. Last night I dreamed again of serpents crawling into my trousers. I've tried on numerous occasions to rid myself of these nightmares, but nothing has worked.

Consulting a psychologist isn't enough. I did that. I've tried a great many things. But the past is inscribed on my body now. When you see the marks on your skin, the scars of torture and cigarette burns, the shape of the chains on your ankles, you feel the past is ineradicable. You carry the marks of the suffering. They're just there. But that's precisely why I carry on with the work of AFESIP.

A lot of people play a part in the work of saving children from sexual slavery, but I feel that some of the volunteers feel a sense of superiority towards the prostituted women. Deep down, they're contemptuous of them. For me it's different, I'm one of them. I share everything they've been through. It's as if we are the same person. I wear their scars on my body and in my soul. We don't need to say much to understand one another. We know that life is a daily hell. Some of the workers here work for their salaries: in their hearts they don't understand.

When I close my eyes I see the physical tortures again. I prefer them to the psychological ones, like those inflicted when I was told my family or my collaborators would be killed. But even so, my eyes close and the blows and kicks are there. Remembering makes you want to die, but you're not allowed to die. You want to disappear, but you can't disappear.

The memories that torment me the most are those of rape and the stink of sperm. In brothels they don't change the sheets very often. The smell of sperm is everywhere. It's insufferable. Even today I have the sense that I'm breathing in the smell of the whorehouses. The customers were dirty. They never showered. I remember one man, who had the most hideous breath. We had no toothpaste but we would brush our teeth with ash or sand. Some of the clients never bothered at all; their teeth were yellow and rotting.

I lived amidst this stench for so long that I can't bear it now. Even fifteen years later I feel dirtied by it. The smell is still in my nostrils. So I wash myself like a madwoman and cover myself in eau de toilette in order to mask the sperm stench that pursues me. At home I have a cupboard full of perfume. I spend money to blot out a smell which probably only exists in my fevered imagination. I chase it away with the contents of my bottles.

Writing this book, I can no longer sleep. It makes me sick. I have nightmares remembering all the horrors. I don't know if I can live my whole life with them. There are times when I'd like to get rid of this burden of memory which weighs me down, which enacts the roll call of my misery, which forces me to have shower after shower, rubbing myself down as hard as possible before covering myself in cream and drowning myself in perfume. What's the use of such an existence? Apart from crying, what does one do with it? Are my friends who have died, and so are free of it all at last, luckier than I am, trapped here with the noise of those ghouls that follow me constantly? I would like to live a happy life, but the problems are always there, always in front of us, gaping, demanding our energy, our ceaseless activity and even our despair! To say that the past is past, that you need to put it all behind you, is what I say all the time to the girls who come to the centre with their unendurable suffering.

I know how to say all this, but I also know it's useless and serves little purpose. Nothing can cauterise those old wounds. If I confide in my husband or my close friend, telling them that I feel dirty, they tell me it's not true, that for them I am this, that, or the other, but I'm not dirty. These words don't help me at all. The only people to whom I can say that I feel dirty and who can understand are the girls who have gone to the same lengths as I have.

Journalists make it difficult, in a way. I am very grateful to them because the attention of the world's newspapers partly saved our cause from being shut down. But often reporters want a 'sexy' project, something hot, to wake up the readers and viewers. They ask me to talk about my past – if not, how will they convey the importance of the work we're doing?

That's one of the reasons I decided to write this book. Perhaps it will stop me having to tell my story over and over again. Another reason is that I want everyone to know what is happening to the women of Cambodia, because one day I may no longer be here. Given what's going on in my country, who knows who may still be alive tomorrow.

When we started doing our work, we couldn't manage to close down the small brothels. We didn't have enough experience and the pimps just laughed at us. Then, with time, work, and support, we began doing it. Now it's the big brothels that pose the challenge.

We have to proceed step by step. We've been working for ten years but it's only in the last three years that we've begun cooperating well with the police. The justice system is beginning to improve too. When there's an AFESIP case these days some of them are more careful because they know we don't let things drop easily. And some people in government do help me: if we had no support from anyone in government none of our work would be possible.

I never wanted to become a public person; it just happened that way. My dream, really, is to be like that old man with the frogs and the King: I would like to have a quiet life, in a garden, living with all my children and with the girls from Thloc Chhroy. I would be a grandmother and great-grandmother and I would be happy, and someone else would have taken over the work of running everything.

But so far it hasn't been like that, and I have written this book for several reasons. I want people to realise to what extent prostitutes are victims and how important it is to help them. These women and girls are marked by their experiences for life, and it will be very hard for .them ever to find even a little happiness. It simply isn't true, as some people think, that girls are glad to find work, that they volunteer for it, that they are well paid.

People think prostitutes are deceitful, dishonest. They think these girls are hard and intractable – we have a saying in Cambodia: 'Don't try to bend the *sroleuw* tree, don't try to change a whore.' On the contrary, prostitutes are often honest girls from the countryside and most of them will do anything they can to leave the suffering they endure in the brothels.

I'd like to say, in this book, that my story isn't important. The point is not what happened to me. I'm writing about it to make visible the lives of so many thousands of other women. They have no voice, so let this one life stand for their story.

On their behalf, I would like this book to serve as a call to the governments of the world to get involved in the battle against the sexual exploitation of women and children. Victims are victims in every country.

I recently set up a foundation that I hope will assist our work. I want to be able to buy enough land so that one day the girls from our Thloc Chhroy centre, who have grown up with us, can all farm it all together. AFESIP is about short-term help: we cannot aid any one girl indefinitely. We cannot pay to educate her beyond a certain level, or allow her to stay on eternally, even though we may be her only family. Our new Foundation will be longer-term and it could help other women – former prostitutes, but also orphans, ethnic minorities, the elderly. We have called it the Somaly Mam Foundation, because my notoriety helps us raise money, but I hope it will be the victims themselves who run it.

For the moment our opponents are winning the war but we've won one battle at least. They've lost face and respect. We've investigated this traffic, shown it for what it is, made it shameful. We've shown that these people aren't invulnerable. I'm glad we've managed that.

People ask me how I can bear to keep doing what I do. I'll tell you. It's the evil that was done to me that propels me on. Is there any other way to exorcise it?

Acknowledgements

I would like to thank all the people who have accompanied my work and who have given their time, their heart and their energy to help me and AFESIP in our combat. Among them, I have a special debt of gratitude to Aru rith; Mr Chheng; Ros Sokha; Emma Bonino; Emmanuel Colineau; my mother, who has taught me so much; Anne Daurelle; Renée Daurelle; Pierre Falavier; Ernesto Carlos Gerardo; Her Majesty Queen Sofia; Jacques Milland; Mariane Pearl; the staff of the Anti-Trafficking Unit of the US State Department; and to Robert Deutsch.

I would also like to thank the people who have helped this book happen: Alain Carrière, my French publisher, who I look on as an adopted grandfather; Ruth Marshall, who gave me the confidence I needed to find these words; and my literary agents, Katrin Hodapp, who I look on as my little sister, and Susanna Lea, whose passion for women's causes I greatly admire.

To my dearest friends, Hun Kimleng, Sophear, Om Yentieng, So Sophal, Her Excellency You Sonlong, Vathani and Seriphan, I want to say how grateful I am for their love and support.

I wish to thank my adoptive family, who took me into their hearts and taught me the values of silence, honesty and hard work. Without them nothing that I have managed to do could have been achieved. Above all, I wish to thank my three children for their patience and for teaching me how to love.

DESERT DAWN

Waris Dirie

Fashion model, UN ambassador and courageous spirit, Waris Dirie is a remarkable woman, born into a family of tribal desert nomads in Somalia. She told her story – enduring female circumcision at five years old; running away at twelve through the desert to escape an arranged marriage; being discovered as she worked as a cleaner in London; and becoming a top fashion model – in her book, the worldwide bestseller, *Desert Flower*.

Although Waris Dirie fled Somalia, she never forgot the country that moulded her. She traces the roots of her courage, resilience and humour back to her culture, and most particularly to her mother.

This is the moving story of her return to Somalia – *Desert Dawn* is about coming home.

'I wanted to return to the place where I was born and see it with new eyes. I had no idea where my family was in Somalia. At first it seemed impossible - almost as impossible as a camel girl becoming a fashion model . . .'

IN THE NAME OF HONOUR

Mukhtar Mai

Mukhtar Mai came to prominence in June 2002, when journalists in Pakistan first learned of her court-ordered gang rape, punishment for an 'honour crime' allegedly committed by her brother, an offence for which there was never any proof.

After the horrific rape, custom dictated that she would kill herself. But Mai defied custom. In an unprecedented act of courage, she took her rapists to court and won.

In this rousing and moving account, Mai describes her experiences and readers get a rare look inside a world of ancient tribal justice, rampant illiteracy, poverty, and economic and sexual bondage.

Mukhtar Mai pitted herself against the system, with extraordinary courage and strength of purpose. Timely and topical, *In the Name of Honour* is the inspirational true story of a woman who fought and triumphed against exceptional odds. Today Mukhtar Mai runs her village's first ever school for girls – seeded with money awarded to her by the Pakistani government in her historic settlement – and is an eager pupil there herself.

www.virago.co.uk

virago

To find out more about Somaly Mam and
other Virago authors, visit:
www.virago.co.uk

Visit the Virago website for:

- Exclusive features and interviews with authors,
  including Margaret Atwood, Maya Angelou,
  Sarah Waters and Nina Bawden

- News of author events and forthcoming titles

- Competitions

- Exclusive signed copies

- Discounts on new publications

- Book-group guides

- Free extracts from a wide range of titles

PLUS: subscribe to our free monthly newsletter

You can order other Virago titles through our website: *www.virago.co.uk* or by using the order form below

☐ Desert Flower	Waris Dirie	£7.99
☐ Desert Dawn	Waris Dirie	£7.99
☐ Desert Children	Waris Dirie	£7.99
☐ In the Name of Honour	Muktar Mai	£10.99

The prices shown above are correct at time of going to press. However, the publishers reserve the right to increase prices on covers from those previously advertised, without further notice.

_____ 🐀 _____

Please allow for postage and packing: **Free UK delivery.**
Europe: add 25% of retail price; Rest of World: 45% of retail price.

To order any of the above or any other Virago titles, please call our credit card orderline or fill in this coupon and send/fax it to:

Virago, PO Box 121, Kettering, Northants NN14 4ZQ
Fax: 01832 733076   Tel: 01832 737526
Email: aspenhouse@FSBDial.co.uk

☐ I enclose a UK bank cheque made payable to Virago for £ . . . .
☐ Please charge £ . . . . . . to my Visa/Delta/Maestro

Expiry Date [| | | |]   Maestro Issue No. [| |]

NAME (BLOCK LETTERS please) . . . .

ADDRESS . . . .

. . . .

. . . .

Postcode . . . . Telephone . . . .

Signature . . . .

Please allow 28 days for delivery within the UK. Offer subject to price and availability.

DESERT FLOWER

Waris Dirie

'A story that traverses continents, spans worlds of human
experience and human pain . . . Waris Dirie was a victim
once, but she never will be again. She is still fighting, still
using her beauty and courage to take what she has learned
to try and put things right'
Sunday Express

'She was circumcised at five, fled an arranged marriage at
twelve, then became a Pirelli girl in her teens. Now, Waris
Dirie is an ambassador for the UN'
Observer

'Born a Somalian nomad, by the time she made it as a top
model, she'd survived genital mutilation and a face-off with
a tiger . . . She's now a UN special Ambassador. Take a cue
from Waris's charm and courage'
Company